The Super Easy Keto Desserts Cookbook

Quick & Easy 5-Ingredients, Mouth-watering Sweets &
Treats that Busy and Novice can Cook
LOOSE UP TO 24 POUNDS

By

Dr. Clay Skinner

INTRODUCTION

Ketogenic diet is the longer name for 'Keto Diet'. It is a type of diet which is modified to be high in fat and at the same time low in carbohydrate. It consists of almost no source of carbohydrate-dense foods and over eighty percent fat. The idea behind this is to make the body to get calories from fats and protein and little or no calories from carbohydrate sources. It serves as a non-drug therapy that helps to shed weight, lower the cholesterol level, boost energy and also to treat other types of diseases like epilepsy, cancer and Alzheimer's disease.

It works by increasing the intake of fatty foods and reducing carbohydrate intake. This reduction in carbohydrate intake puts the body into a state called ketosis (a metabolic state). In this condition, the body burns fat instead of carbohydrate to generate energy. In the liver, this mechanism also helps to turn fats into ketone. This can help supply energy for and also to the brain.

Keto diet helps in altering how the body gets energy from food. Normally, carbohydrate is broken down during digestion. Carbohydrates, when digested are broken down into smaller, simple sugars like glucose, galactose, and fructose. Glucose serves as the main source of energy for the body. When glucose cannot be gotten from the body for energy (this happens either when an individual has not eaten in a long while or when carbohydrates which help to produce glucose, is absent from the diet, as in the case of keto diets), it begins to look for other ways to get energy (as in the case of keto diet where it uses fat). This action puts the body in a ketosis state (a process where there is a release of fat from the cells of the body and this fat is turned in to ketone bodies). These ketones are the 'plan B' of the body to generate energy.

In general, the keto diet lowers the level of insulin present in the body and also lowers the level of blood sugar by shifting the metabolism of the body towards ketones and fats and away from carbohydrates.

Origin of the Keto Diet (low carb and high fat)

The keto diet has been in place for nearly a hundred years. Researchers on epilepsy found out that fewer seizures were noticed in patients that their body level of ketones was increased. This was found out in the 1920s. Asides from been useful in the treatment of epilepsy, there are pieces of evidence to support that keto diets have therapeutic effects on other diseases like cancer, diabetics, neurological conditions, polycystic ovary syndrome among many others.

Keto diets have also been known to have a great track record in weight loss and they have been used as a recipe for weight loss for over three decades (thirty years).

BENEFITS OF THE KETO DIET

Knowing the benefits of keto diets helps one see how it can help to reduce weight safely. Below are the benefits of keto diets.

1. Keto diets help in weight loss

Keto diets help in loss of weight in two ways;

a. By increasing the number of calories needed to generate energy

It helps weight loss by increasing the number of calories needed to generate energy. This is so because the body does more work in turning fats to energy than in turning carbohydrates to energy. By putting the body in a state of ketosis, the calories that should have contributed to body weight (in a normal diet) is used to turn fat to energy (as in a keto diet).

b. By reducing appetite

Keto diets lead to weight loss by reducing appetites, thereby reducing the amount of food eaten and subsequently preventing weight gain. Food cravings are controlled by controlling the level of the blood sugar.

Because the ketogenic diet is also high in protein and fat, it does not make one hungry quickly. Because of this, there is a low/reduced intake of calories in turn leads to a weight loss.

2. Keto diets lead to a loss of stomach fat

Stomach/belly fat is a great concern nowadays, not only for health reasons, but also for fashion, social acceptance.

The distribution of fat in the body affects risks of some diseases. For example, excess visceral fat (fat around the abdomen) increases the risk of diabetics. Keto diets are very effective to reduce visceral fat (abdominal fat). A large proportion of the fat people lose while on keto diets are the abdominal fats that are harmful and that cause metabolic disorder that are harmful.

3. Reduction in the Risk of cardiovascular Diseases

Due to the reduction in viscera fat by keto diet, there is a reduction in the risk of cardio vascular diseases such as hypertension, heart disease. Also, keto diets help to lower the blood pressure and this in turn leads to a reduction in the risk of cardiovascular diseases.

4. Keto diets help to reduce the number of Triglycerides.

Triglycerides are a type of fat that is found in the blood. They are the most abundant fat in the body. As much as they are important for health, they are harmful (because they actually increase the risk of heart disease). Hence, a control of the level of triglycerides in the body should be optimal so as to promote good health.

High carbohydrate consumption is one of the causes of a high triglyceride profile, especially in people that are sedentary or have a low activity level. So, when people are on a low carbohydrate diet (as in people on keto diet), their triglyceride level begins to drop, thereby reducing the amount of triglyceride in the body.

5. Reduction in Acnes Out Break

One of the causes of out breaks of acnes is related to the level of the sugar in the blood and also the diet. A regular intake of a diet that has high amounts of refined and processed carbohydrate makes the gut bacteria to be altered. It (high intake of refined and processed carbohydrates) also cause fluctuations in the level of blood sugar. These can have not desirable effects on the skin health and lead to a break out of acnes.

Therefore, seeing that a keto diet is a low carb diet, then it can help reduce the break out of acnes.

6. Keto Diet may help to Reduce the Risk of Cancer

As a by influence of the keto diet reducing insulin complications by reducing high blood sugar level, it helps to reduce the risk of some cancers when used in combination with radiation and chemo therapy.

7. Keto Diet helps to Increase the Level of High-Density Lipoprotein.

High density lipoprotein is most times referred to as the good cholesterol. The higher the level of high-density lipoprotein as compared to the level of low-density lipoprotein, the lower the risk of heart disease.

Eating fat is a very good way of increasing the level of high-density lipoproteins. So, high density lipoprotein levels increase while on high fat, low carb diet (an example being keto diet).

8. Keto Diets reduce the risk of Diabetics

Keto diets are very helpful for diabetes patients and other patients with insulin resistance. Cutting carbohydrates in the diet helps to lower the blood sugar level and also the level of insulin in the body.

9. Keto Diets help are Therapeutic in treating certain Brain disorders

The brain burns glucose as fuel, so even if the body isn't getting enough carbohydrates, it produces the needed glucose from proteins eaten. Yet, the brain can also get fuel by burning the ketones formed when the intake of carbohydrate is low or during starvation. This process has protective abilities on neurological conditions. This can be used to prevent or treat certain conditions like Alzheimer's condition and also Parkinson's disease.

INGREDIENTS, TOOLS AND RECIPES IN THE KETO DIET

1. Meat (pork, bacon, ham, lamb, steak, chicken, beef, turkey and other meats)
2. Dairy that are high in fat (like cheese, heavy cream)
3. Fats and Oils Generally (vegetable oil, avocado oil, coconut oil, olive oil, butter, lard)
4. Nuts (walnuts, ground nuts, almond, peanuts)
5. Eggs
6. A little bit of alcohol
7. Some vegetables that are high in fat (e.g. zucchini, mushroom, lettuce, cabbage, olives)

Keto Desserts

Keto desserts are desserts on the keto diet meal plan. They have all the advantages of the keto diet since they are a type of the dirt itself.

Tools Needed for Keto Desserts Preparation

1. Instant pots: it is great for cooking and boiling the ingredients on the keto lists.
2. Pie pans: it is used to make buns, bread.
3. Silicone baking mats: they help in baking pizzas, cheese crisp etc.
4. Milk frothier: it is used to make bulletproof coffee (an important staple on the keto diet list)
5. Silicone muffin liners: it can be used to make fat bombs
6. Cast iron skillet: it is very useful in preparing steaks and burgers.
7. Spiralizer: it is used to spiralize zucchini, egg plants, broccoli stalks and the likes.
8. Blender: It can be used to make homemade mayonnaise, pancake mixtures and also protein shakes.
9. Food scale
10. Burger Press: it is used to get uniformity while making burgers
11. Grill: it is used to grill chicken, turkey and other means.

12. Butter bell: it is used to store butter safely at room temperature.
13. Jars with lids: it is used to store food
14. Mandolin slicer: it is used to slice ingredients. It also can be used to make veggie ribbons.
15. Slow cooker: ii is used to cook recipe slowly.
16. Oil mister: it helps to have an even spray of oil and also to prevent the clogging of oil.
17. Cookie scoop: it is used to scoop cookies in a regular shape and size and also to scoop other foods on the keto diet list that requires a perfect shape and size.
18. Paring knife: it is very sharp and is used to cut almost any ingredient on the keto diet list.
19. Whipped cream whipper (homemade): it is used to prepare whipped cream at home.
20. Measuring spoons
21. Greater
22. Kitchen mats
23. Mixing bowls
24. Baking dish
25. Avocado saver: it helps to keep the avocado from burning

Keto Dessert's Recipes

BARS

1. Keto Peanut Butter Bars

Nutritional value of a serving (1 bar)

- Total calories: 112 calories
- Fat: 8 g
- Carbohydrates: 4 g

- Protein: 4 g
- Fiber: 3g

Serving size: 20 bars

Preparation time: 5 minutes

Ingredients:

- Half a cup of coconut flour
- Two cups of peanut butter that is smooth
- Half cup of sweetener that is sticky

Preparation

- Place a parchment paper in a square pan and line it with it
- Put all the ingredients into a big mixing bowl and mix until it is fully combined
- Pour the batter into the already lined baking pan and refrigerate it till it is firm.
- When it is firm, cut it into 20 bars and serve.

2. Keto Chocolate crunch Bars

They are paleo and vegan friendly.

Nutritional value of a serving (a bar)

- Total Calories: 155 calories
- Fat: 12 g
- Carbohydrate: 4 g

- Protein: 7 g
- Fiber: 2 g

Serving size: 20 bars

Preparation Time: 5 minutes

Ingredients

- One and a half cup of chocolate chips (of choice)
- One cup of almond butter (or any seed/nut butter of choice)
- A quarter cup of coconut oil
- Half cup of sweetener that is sticky
- Three cups of almond nuts or cashew nuts (or any other nuts you desire)

Preparation

- Get a big baking dish and line it with parchment paper.
- Get a bowl that is microwave friendly and mix the chocolate chips, the coconut oil, the almond butter and the sweetener and melt them till they combine.
- Then add the almond nut or the cashew nut or your desired nuts and combine the mixture well by mixing it.
- Pour the mixture into the already lined baking dish and let it spread.
- Refrigerate the mixture till it is firm. When it is firm, cut it into 20 bars and serve.

3. Keto Coconut Chocolate Bars

This is a great easy to make chocolate bar on the keto dessert list. It does not require sugar, does not require baking and has just five minutes of preparation time.

Nutritional value of a serving (a bar)

- Total calories: 106
- Calories from fat: 99
- Total fat: 11 g
- Total carbohydrates: 3 g
- Protein: 2 g

Portion size: 20 bars   Preparation Time: 5 minutes

Ingredients

- Two cups of any type of chocolate chips desired
- One cup of coconut oil that is melted
- Three cups of coconut flakes that is shredded
- A quarter cup of sweetener

Preparation

- Use a parchment paper to line the inside of a big baking pan.
- Get a big mixing bowl and put all of the ingredients. Mix the mixture to let it be well combined
- Pour the batter (the mixture) in the already lined with parchment paper pan. Use your hands to press it firmly. Wet your hands to press it.
- Refrigerate to make it firm. When it is firm, remove from the refrigerator and cut it into 20 bars and put it back in the refrigerator.
- Melt the chocolate chips and dip each of the coconut bars into the melted chocolate. Refrigerate again and serve.

4. Keto Lemon Bars

This is a great dessert option on the keto menu list because it has a high taste of sweet lemon and also provides vitamin c.

Nutritional value of a serving (a bar)

- Calories: 193 calories
- Fat: 19 g

- Protein: 4 g
- Carbohydrates: 3 g

Serving size: 8 servings (8 bars)   Preparation Time: 30 minutes

Ingredients

- Three lemons
- One and a half cup of almond flour
- Half a cup of butter
- One cup of powdered sweetener

Preparation

- Get a baking dish and line it with parchment paper.
- Mix a cup of the almond flour, a quarter of the sweetener, the butter and a pinch of salt together in a medium mixing bowl. Pour this mixture into the baking dish that is

already lined with parchment paper and bake for about 20 minutes. Remove and let it cool down.

- Zest one of the lemons in a medium bowl and juice the three lemons. Put the eggs and the rest of the sweetener, the rest of the almond flour and add a pinch of salt. Mix together to make the filling.
- This filling can now be poured into the baked crust and bake for 15 minutes.
- Remove and serve with slices of lemon. Also sprinkle sweetener on it.

5. Chocolate chip pumpkin protein bar

This keto protein bar is also gluten free and paleo asides from being keto. So, it is three in on.

Nutritional Value in a Serving

- Calories: 89.1 calories
- Fat: 2.7 g

- Protein: 7.1 g
- Carbohydrate: 5.7 g

Serving size: 8 bars

Preparation time: 5 minutes

Ingredients

- Two table spoons of chocolate chips that is sugar free
- Half a cup of coconut flour
- Three table spoons of protein powder
- Half a cup of pumpkin puree
- One table spoon of pumpkin pie spice
- Three table spoons of butter powder
- A pinch of salt
- Half cup of almond milk that is unsweetened
- Two table spoons of powdered sweetener

Preparation

- Get a medium baking pan and line it with parchment paper

- Get a medium mixing bowl; add the butter powder flour, the protein powder, a pinch of salt, the coconut flour, the powdered sweetener and the pumpkin pie spice. Mix together until they are well combined.
- Add the pumpkin puree and the almond milk and stir well until they have combined well. Also add the chocolate chips and stir.
- Pour the mixture into the baking pan and make it firm by pressing it down.
- Refrigerate for some minutes and slice in to bars, then serve.

6. Vanilla Keto Waffles

Delicate and satisfying vanilla keto waffles will be an excellent breakfast or dinner. The gentle taste of vanilla, the pleasant aroma of hot fresh waffles will be able to cheer you up all day or evening.

Nutritional value of serving:
- Total Calories: 242
- Protein: 8 grams
- Fats: 12 grams
- Pure carbohydrates: 4 grams

Cooking time: 5 minutes

Servings Per Container:

Ingredients:
- Coconut Flour - 4 Tbsp
- Egg white - 4 pieces
- Milk (almond, almond, etc.) - 25 ml
- Apple or pumpkin puree - 1 tablespoon
- Coconut oil - 1 tablespoon
- Ground Cinnamon - ¼ teaspoon
- Dough baking powder - ¼ teaspoon
- Vanilla extract - to your taste

Preparation of vanilla keto waffles
- vanilla keto waffles with syrup
- Combine coconut flour, ground cinnamon, salt, erythritol, baking powder and vanilla extract in a large bowl
- In another bowl mix milk, coconut oil and white egg. Stir properly until the ingredients are smooth

- For the liquid ingredients, add a dry mixture of flour gradually and spices.
- Mix the dough until it is smooth.
- The dough is to be prepared thick, but not too dense (you should be comfortable mixing it). In case the dough is too thick, add ½ tablespoon of drinking water to it;
- Let the dough stand for 10-15 minutes;
- Preheat the waffle iron and spread the dough over all the recesses. Bake the waffles for 4-6 minutes (depending on the installed capacity of the waffle iron).
- Put ready-made keto waffles on a plate and decorate with syrup
- Ready-made waffles can be served immediately after baking. They can also be put in the refrigerator, and then heated with a toaster before serving. Sometimes these keto waffles are tastier than freshly baked.

7. Almond flour keto waffles

Almond flour has reduced carbohydrate content and absolutely no gluten. In addition, the nut itself has a lot of healthy vitamin E and magnesium. The keto waffles made with Almond flour have a pleasant nutty aroma and unusual texture. You can make this ingredient yourself, grinding nuts, or having bought in a specialized store. Be sure to beat the egg whites as you are cooking. This would make your keto waffles light and airy. This style can be used in making Belgian waffles.

In the place of butter, you can use peanut or coconut oil. It all depends on your preference.

Preparation time: 20 minutes   Portion Size: 2 servings

Ingredients:
- Chicken eggs: 4 pieces
- Almond flour: 2 cups (500 ml)
- Granulated Sweetener - ¼ cup (60 ml)
- Dough baking powder - 2 teaspoons
- Salt - 1 teaspoon
- Butter - 125 ml
- Almond oil - 125 ml
- Vanilla Extract - 2 teaspoons

Preparation
- Combine almond flour, sweetener, baking powder and salt in a deep bowl;
- Melt the butter and almond butter in the microwave;

- Mix melted butter and almond butter with flour and other dry ingredients;
- Add the yolks and vanilla extract to the mixture;
- Beat the eggs until whites in a separate bowl until stable peaks.
- Transfer the whipped proteins to the batter and mix everything gently;
- Preheat the waffle iron. Cook waffles for 5 minutes.
- Keto waffles will be ready when they have a golden crust.

8. Keto Chocolate Peppermint Cookie Bars

Nutritional Value of a serving (a Bar)

- Total Calories: 123
- Fat: 11 g
- Carbohydrate :7.3 g
- Protein: 5 g
- Fiber: 2.2 g
- Iron 6 mg

Preparation Time: 30 minutes

Serving Size: 10 servings (10 bars)

Ingredients:

For the chocolate drizzle

- One table spoon of granulated sweetener
- One table spoon of vanilla extract
- Two table spoons of cocoa powder
- Three table spoons of melted coconut oil

For the cookie bars

- Three cups of shredded coconut
- 6 tablespoons of protein powder
- Two table spoons of granulated sweetener
- One table spoon of pepper mint oil
- A pinch of salt
- Two table spoons of vanilla extract

Preparation

- Get a loaf pan and line it with parchment paper.
- Put the shredded coconut in a blender and blend on high speed. Add the remaining ingredients for the cookie bar and also blend on high speed till the mixture is fully combined.

- Pour the mixture into the already lined loaf pan and use a spoon to press it down well. Then freeze it for about 30 minutes.
- To prepare the chocolate drizzle, add all the ingredients for the chocolate drizzle in a small bowl and mix them until they have combined fully well.
- Remove the pan and remove the cookie from the pan, then slice into 10 bars.
- Dip the cookie inside the chocolate mixture, remove and freeze for about 5 more minutes.
- Serve cold

9. Keto Coconut Macadamia Bars

Nutritional Value of a serving (a bar)

- Total calories: 199
- Calories from Fat: 174
- Carbohydrates: 4.3 g
-
- Fat: 19.3 g
- Protein: 3.1 g

Serving size: 15 bars

Preparation Time: 1 hour

Ingredients

For the crust

- A cup of almond flour
- A quarter cup of chilled butter
- A pinch of salt
- Half a cup of powdered sweetener

For the filling

- A quarter cup of butter
- One cup of chopped macadamia nuts
- Half cup of coconut cream
- Half cup of powdered sweetener
- One egg yolk
- One and a half cup of flaked coconut
- Half table spoon of vanilla extract

Preparation

For the crust

- First of all, heat the oven to 350F.
- Mix the almond flour, the sweetener, and the salt in a food processor. Pour the butter inside and pulse until the mixture turns fine crumbs.
- Pour the mixture from where it is into a square baking pan (of 8 inches) and bake until it is golden brown. This should take about 15 minutes. Remove the pan from the oven and let it cool while you make the filling

For the filling

- Place a small sauce pan on medium heat; add the butter to get it melted.
- Then put in the remaining ingredients for the filling and stir until they have combined well.
- Pour the filling on the crust and bake for 30 minutes. Remove it and let it get cooled before you cut it into bars.

10.   Cocoa Keto Bars

Nutritional value of a serving (a bar)

Total Calories: 216   Preparation Time: 40 minutes

Serving Size: 12 bars

Ingredients

For the coconut layer (bottom)

- Two cups of shredded coconut that is unsweetened
- One table spoon of sweetener
- Half cup of melted coconut oil

For the chocolate topping layer

- One table spoon of coconut oil
- Two table spoons of granulated sweetener
- One cup of unsweetened chocolate

Preparation

For the coconut layer

- Add all the ingredients for the coconut layer into a food processor and process until the mixture is well combined.
- Press the combined mixture into the bottom of a silicon pan and refrigerate while the topping is being prepared.

For the Chocolate Layer

- Melt the coconut and chocolate together in a microwave. Add the sweetener and stir.
- Spread this chocolate layer on the coconut layer evenly and freeze for 30 minutes.
- Remove and cut into bars and serve.

CAKES

11. Keto Flourless Chocolate Cake

Keto chocolate cake is rich and delicious. It is good for a low carb dessert that is high in fat (keto dessert). It does not require flour (in accordance to the low carb rule of the keto diet), yet it has a very unimaginable soft texture. It also has an intense rich chocolate flavor; it is dense and very great for parties and other celebrations. There are different varieties of the flourless chocolate cake as it accommodates people on vegan diet and also people on gluten free diet.

- Vegan Keto Flourless Chocolate Cake

For a vegan keto diet, use egg replacer instead of egg. Mix the egg replacer with some water and allow it to get thickened by allowing it to stand for a few minutes. Also be sure to use a plant-based milk.

- Gluten Free Keto Flourless Cake

A gluten free keto flourless chocolate cake is sweetened with either coconut sugar or date sugar or erythritol instead of the normal regular sugar.

Serving Size: 4 portions

Preparation Time: 30 minutes

Ingredients

- One and a half cup of cocoa powder
- Two table spoons of baking powder
- Two and a half spoons of Dutch cocoa
- One and a half cup of milk (use a plant-based milk like coconut milk, almond milk or other plant-based milk of choice for the vegan version of the keto flourless chocolate cake)
- One and a half table spoon of flavor of choice
- One cup of sugar (coconut sugar or date sugar of half of a cup of erythritol for the gluten free version)

Tools/utensils needed

- Oven
- Baking pan
- Parchment paper to line the baking pan
- Big mixing bowl
- Small mixing bowl
- Big spoon or spatula

Preparation

- First of all, heat the oven to about 350F
- Get a baking pan and line it with the parchment paper
- In a big mixing bowl, mix all the dry ingredients (the cocoa powder, the Dutch cocoa, the baking powder, the coconut sugar or the date sugar
- Use a mixer to whisk the eggs. Do this till the size has doubled and till it is frothy.
- In another small mixing bowl, mix the wet ingredients (the milk and the flavor)
- Gently add the mixed wet ingredients to the mixed dry ingredients and stir.
- Pour the mixture into the already lined baking pan with parchment paper.
- Bake for about 30 minutes.
- Remove from baking pan and serve

12. Brownie Cheese Cake

Brownie cheese cake is a combination of cheese cake (low in carbohydrate) and brownies that are gluten free. So, it is two delicious desserts in one! The amount of carb in this is less than 0.5g per serving.

Ingredients

- Almond flour or coconut flour (that is finely ground)
- Butter (soft): grass fed butter should be used because it contains more healthy fats (omega 3 fatty acids) and has a higher micronutrient level than regular butter. Also, to make the butter soft, keep the butter for about 40 minutes at room temperature. This helps to reduce the strength and thickness of the butter and make it soft.
- Erythritol (the powdered form): this sweetener is used in keto desserts because it is keto diet friendly as it does not raise the blood sugar level and it is very safe to use.

- Cocoa powder: Dutch baking cocoa powder): it is used because just a small amount is needed to achieve a great chocolate taste and flavor and helps to achieve a low carbohydrate recipe.
- Vanilla extract (that is free of sugar)
- Cream cheese (the full fat type)
- Some chocolate bars (to be grated)

Tools/ utensils used

- Fridge/ freezer
- Parchment paper to line the silicon molds
- Mixing bowls
- Big spoon
- Greater
- Silicon molds

Preparation

For the brownie layer

- Mix the Dutch baking cocoa powder and the vanilla extract in a mixing bowl until it has combined well
- Add the soft butter and mix well. (be sure to make the butter mix well in the mixture to form a paste)
- Pour the mixture (the brownie layer) halfway into an appropriate silicon mold of the desired size (be sure to fill it halfway to allow for the cheese layer to also be poured in it)
- The brownie layer can be stored in a fridge pending the time the cheesecake layer would be ready.

For the cheese cake layer

- Add the rest of the butter, the almond flour or coconut flour, the rest of the vanilla essence into a mixing bowl and mix till it is very smooth.

- When it is very smooth, pour the mixture into the cooled half-filled silicon mold till it is filled up.

- Freeze in a freezer for about 2 hours or till it is hard enough.

- Remove the already made brownie cheesecake from the silicon mold carefully and serve.

13.   Peanut Butter Molten Lava Cake

Nutrition Content in a Serving (one medium sized cake)

- Total Calories: 387 Calories
- Calories from fat: 315 Calories
- Total Fat: 35.02g
- Cholesterol: 215 mg
- Protein :10.44g
- Carbohydrate :6.41
- Fiber: 1.13g

Serving size: 4 servings (4 cakes)   Preparation Time: 25 minutes

Ingredients

- 2 very big eggs and their yolks
- A cup of peanut butter
- Chocolate sauce (that is low carb)
- Six full table spoons of almond flour
- one full table spoons of vanilla essence
- two table spoons of coconut oil
- seven tablespoons of sweetener (powered form)
- a spoon of butter to grease the baking pan

Tools/ utensils needed

- oven
- baking pan
- mixing bowls
- bowl that is microwave safe
- spoons
- knife

Preparation

- Heat the oven to about 370F
- Use the butter to grease the baking pan very well so that the cake would remove smoothly without any dent.
- Put the coconut oil and peanut butter into a bowl that is microwave safe and stir.
- Heat them for a little while to get it melted. When the mixture is already melted, stir it well till it mixes together and is smooth.
- Add the powdered sweetener into the melted mixture and whisk it. Also add the almond flour, the vanilla essence, the eggs and their yolks. Shake and mix together the mixture until it is very smooth.
- Fill the baking pan with the barter and bake for about 15 minutes.
- Once done, remove the cake from the pan using a knife to loosen the cake from the baking pan.
- Place on a serving plate and drizzle it with the chocolate sauce (that is low in carbohydrate)
- Follow this process for the four cakes

14.   Chocolate Japanese Cheesecake

This is the chocolate version of the Japanese cotton cheesecake. The recipe is a bit simpler than the standard one, but the result is simply excellent. In the cheesecake there is no flour and sugar, and in one portion, there is only 2 g of carbohydrates.

Nutritional value of one serving
- Calories from Fat: 135 Calories
- Fat: 11 g
- Carbohydrate: 6 g
- Fiber: 4 g
- Digestible Carbohydrate: 2 g
- Protein: 4 g

Preparation Time: 40 min   Serving size: 8

Ingredients

- Egg: 3 pieces
- Cream Cheese (Philadelphia): 120 g
- Sugar Free Chocolate: 100 g
- Lemon juice: 1/2 tsp

Preparation

- Preheat your oven to 170 ° C (top and bottom heat, without convection) and place a pan with water on the bottom. Cover the bottom and sides of the 20 cm baking dish with parchment and grease it with oil; Wrap foil outside.
- Separate the whites from the yolks. Beat the proteins at low speed until foam; add lemon juice and beat at high speed until steady peaks.
- Melt your chocolate in water bath, add cream cheese to it and mix until smooth. Remove from heat, cool slightly, add yolks and mix thoroughly.
- Gently add the proteins to the chocolate mixture (one-third at a time), mix and pour the dough into a baking dish.
- Place the pan directly on a baking sheet with water and cook for 15 minutes. Then lower the temperature to 150 ° C and cook for another 20 minutes. Turn off the oven and leave the cheesecake in it for another 20 minutes.

15.   Italian Cream Cake

This cake isn't really Italian as the name implies, never the less it is a great cake that is delicious and also yummy.

Serving size: 4 portions

Ingredients

For the Cake

- Two cups of almond flour
- One cup of coconut flour
- One cup of softened butter that is unsalted

- 4 very big eggs
- 1 cup of erythritol
- A pinch of salt
- 2 table spoon of baking powder
- One cup of heavy cream
- Half table spoon of cream of tartar
- One table spoon of vanilla extract
- One cup of pecans (already chopped)
- One cup of already shredded coconut

For the frosting

- Half cup of heavy cream
- One cup of soft butter that is unsalted
- Two table spoons of vanilla extract
- One cup of cream cheese
- Half cup of swerve (powdered)

For the garnish

- Two table spoons of pecans that are chopped already
- Two table spoons of shredded coconut that are toasted

Tools/ utensils

- Oven
- Cake baking pan
- Parchment paper liner
- Mixing bowl

Preparation

- Before starting the preparation, first heat the oven to about 350F
- Use the parchment paper lining to line the inside of the cake baking pan and grease it with a little butter for easy remover

- Add the flour, the baking powder, the salt and the pecans and coconut into a large bowl and stir.
- In another bowl, put the sweetener and the butter and cream it until it becomes very fluffy and light.
- Remove the yolks from the egg and beat them. Then add to the mixture of sweetener and butter and mix it well.
- Then add the heavy cream and the vanilla to the above mixture and mix it very well again.
- Add the dry ingredients (the almond flour, the coconut flour, the salt and the baking powder) in to the mixed butter mixture and stir until it is fully combined.
- Put the egg whites of the already removed yolk into a bowl and whisk it together with the cream of tartar. Mix it well until it foams.
- Then fold this mixture into the already mixed barter. To make the batter light, be sure to fold the egg white mixture lightly.
- Pour the battered mixture into the baking pan and allow it to bake for about 40 minutes in the already heated oven. By this time, the edges of the cake should be a shade of golden brown and the center of the cake should be firm.
- Leave it in the baking pans to cool.
- Remove the cake from the pans when they are already cool.

For the frosting

- Put the cream cheese and the butter together in a mixing bowl and start to mix them until the mixture becomes very fluffy and light.
- To the mixture, add the sweetener and the vanilla and mix it by beating the mixture.
- Next, add the heavy cream to the mixture. To get your desired consistency, add the heavy cream slowly so as to be able to stop when it reaches the desired consistency.
- Paste the top of the cake and the side of the cake with the frosting.
- On the top layer of the cake, sprinkle the roasted coconut that was shredded and use to decorate the cake.

16.   Gooey Butter Cake

Gooey butter cake originated from the United States, from St Louis, Missouri to be precise. The cake is usually dense and flat and also, it usually has a topping of a gooey filling that is sweet and made from butter and cream cheese. The gooey butter cake has three portions: the cake portion, the filling portion and the sprinkling portion. The cake portion is made with a cake mix that is boxed with a lot of added butter, addition of lesser eggs and also no addition of liquids to the cake barter. This is done like that so that it will not rise too much and also so that it will remain buttery and dense. The filling is made by mixing butter, sugar that is in powdered form, cream cheese and egg together by beating it together. Then this mixture is over the top of the cake and then baked till the filling gets gooey. The sprinkling portion is made by sprinkling a desired amount of sugar (or sweetener of choice) on the cake.

Nutrition content

- Total Calories: 268 calories
- Calories from fat: 218 calories
- Fat: 24. 2 g
- Carbohydrates: 4.2 g
- Protein: 6.1 g
- Fiber: 1.6 g

Portion size: 15 servings

Preparation Time: 60 minutes

Ingredients

For the cake

- Two cups of coconut flour (or almond flour))
- One egg
- A little salt
- Half cup of swerve sweetener
- One table spoon of vanilla extract
- Two table spoons of baking powder
- Half cup of butter that is already melted
- Two table spoons of whey protein powder that is not flavored.

For the filling portion

- Two cups of already softened cream cheese
- One table spoon of vanilla extract
- A cup of powdered swerve sweetener
- Two eggs

For the sprinkling portion

- A cop of powdered swerve sweetener

Tools / utensils needed

- Oven
- Baking pan
- Mixing bowls
- Stirrer

Preparation

For the cake portion

- Before starting the preparation process, heat the oven to about 325F
- Grease the inside of the baking pan to be used. Grease it with butter to make the cake remove easily.
- Put the almond /coconut flour, the baking powder, a little salt, the protein powder and the sweetener in a mixing bowl and mix together until it combines. Also, add the egg, the vanilla extract and the butter and mix well till it combines evenly with the mixture. Pour this mixture in to the previously greased baking pan half way.

For the filling

- Mix the butter and cream cheese together in another mixing bowl and mix well by beating them together. Then add the sweetener until it has fully dissolved and combine with the mixture, then add the eggs and vanilla essence till it is very smooth.
- Pour the filling mixture into the half-filled baking pan and bake for about 45 minutes. By this time, the edges of the cake are golden brown in color and the center is still jiggling.
- Take away the cake and allow cooling. Then remove and place in a serving plate.
- Dust or sprinkle the cake with the powdered swerve and cut the cake into equal bars.

17.   Pecan Pie Cheese cake

Nutrition Content

- Total Calories: 340 calories
- Calories from Fat: 279 calories
- Fat: 31.03 g

- Protein: 5.89 g
- Carbohydrate: 4.97 g
- Fiber 1.42

Serving size: 10 servings

Preparation time: 50 minutes +3 hours to chill

Ingredients

For the crust

- A cup of almond flour
- A little salt
- Two table spoons of swerve sweetener in the powdered form
- Two table spoons of melted butter

For the filling (pecan pie)

- Half a cup of already chopped pecans
- One egg
- Half a cup of butter
- A little salt
- A quarter cup of powered serve sweetener
- Two table spoon of whipping cream (heavy)
- One table spoon of vanilla extract or caramel extract

For the topping

- Two table spoons of butter
- One tablespoon of whipping cream (heavy)
- Half a cup of already powdered swerve sweetener
- Two tablespoons of bacon syrup
- Toasted pecans (whole) to garnish the cake

- One table spoon of vanilla extract or caramel extract

For the cheese cake filling

- Half cup of whipping cream (heavy)
- One big egg
- Half table spoon of vanilla extract
- Two cups of softened cream cheese
- Five table spoons of powdered swerve sweeteners

Preparation

For the crust

- Add the almond flour, the salt and the swerve sweetener into a big mixing bowl and whisk together.
- Add the butter that is now melted and stir well until the mixture becomes clumpy.
- Put the mixture into a spring foam pan and press it to the bottom and up the sides of the baking pan part way. Keep in the freezer during the time to prepare the pecan pie filing.

Pecan pie filling

- Melt the butter. This can be done by putting it in a small pot and placing it over low heat. Add the bacon syrup and the sweetener into the melted butter and mix it together until they have combined evenly. Add the vanilla extract or chocolate extract and the heavy whipping cream and stir until they have combined fully.
- Then add the egg and start to cook it until this mixture gets thick. After about a minute, stop cooking the mixture from the heat and add the salt and pecan and then stir well.
- Spread the mixture over the crust's bottom.

For the cheese cake filling

- Put the cream cheese into a bowl and beat it until it becomes smooth. Then add the sweetener, the whipping cream, the vanilla extract and the egg, beating each ingredient as you add each one.
- Pour this mixture on the pecan pie filling and make sure it spreads to the edges.

For the baking

- Use a big piece of foil paper to warp the bottom of the spring form baking pan. On top of the spring form baking pan, out a piece of towel (paper). Be careful so as not to let it touch the cheese cake. Also wrap the foil paper around the top of the pan. The essence of wrapping with foil paper is to prevent excess moisture from entering into the cake barter.
- Bake the cake in an oven for few minutes and remove the cake from the baking pan and let it cool down. After this, place the cooled cake in the refrigerator and refrigerate it for over 3 hours.

For the topping

- Place a small pot over low heat; put the butter in it to get it melted. Then put the bacon syrup and the sweetener, whisk them to make the mixture combine well, then add the vanilla or caramel extract, stir, also add the heavy whipping cream and stir again.
- Drizzle this mixture (the topping) on the cheese cake and use the toasted pecans to garnish it.

18.   Caramel Cake

This cake is basically a vanilla flavored cake that is almond flour based.

Nutritional Content

- Total Calories: 388 calories
- Calories from Fat: 314 calories
- Fat: 34. 9 g
- Protein :9.5 g
- Carbohydrate: 7.6 g
- Fiber; 3.4 g

Serving Size: 3 servings   Preparation Time: 1 hour 10 minutes

<u>Ingredients</u>

- One cup of almond flour
- Three table spoons of coconut flour
- Half a cup of almond milk
- Three table spoons of already softened butter
- Two tablespoons of whey protein flour (the unflavored one)
- A big egg
- A cup of caramel source that does not have sugar
- A pinch of salt
- Half tablespoon of baking powder
- Half table spoon of the vanilla extract

Preparation

To make the cake

- First of all, heat the ovens to about 375F. Take a baking pan and grease it to avoid the cake getting stuck in it during removal. Place the parchment paper in the baking pan and also grease the parchment paper.
- Mix the flours (the almond flour and the coconut flour) in a mixing bowl and whisk in the baking powder, salt and whey protein.
- In another mixing bowl, whisk the sweetener and the eggs together. Stop when the mixture becomes fluffy and white. Beat the butter into the mixture and also beat the vanilla extract in too.
- Add the rest of the ingredients into the barter. Remember to beat the mixture very well upon addition of an ingredient.
- Pour the batter into the cake baking pan and let it spread to the edges of the baking pan. Make sure the top of the batter is smoothened and place the baking pan in the oven.
- Bake the cake till the color of the edges are golden in color and also till the top of the cake becomes firm. This should take about 25 minutes.

- Take away the cake from the baking pan and put in a flat plate for it to cool down. Remove the parchment paper longing if it sticks to the cake.

To make the caramel glaze

- Place a big sauce pan on low heat and prepare two cups of the caramel sauce that is sugar free. A big sauce pan is needed because the caramel sauce would double in size.
- When the sauce is ready, ensure that you allow it to cool down (to room temperature). When it is at room temperature, it would be thicker but you would still be able to pour it. As it cools more, it will become thicker.
- Put the serving plate that has the cake on a table close to you, then pour about a quarter of the caramel sauce on it. Use a spatula to gently spread the caramel sauce to the edges of the cake. Leave it for about 15 minutes so that the sauce can thicken further.
- When the first layer of caramel sauce has thickened, pour another layer, almost all of the rest of the caramel sauce on the cake and allow it to drip down the cake.
- Add the remaining caramel sauce and spread it over the top and the sides of the cake

19.   Kentucky Butter Cake

This type of cake is moist and also contains a butter cake plus a butter sauce that is very sweet and soaks the cake. The major ingredient in this cake is butter. A very large amount of butter is needed to make this cake. The difference between the normal Kentucky butter cake and the keto version is the type of flour used. In the keto version, almond flour is used as against the wheat flour used in the normal version.

Nutrition content of a serving

- Total calories; 301 calories
- Calories from fat; 244 calories
- Fat; 27.07 g

- Carbohydrate; 5.54 g
- Protein; 7.34 g
- Fiber; 2.4 g

Serving Size: 4 servings

Preparation time: 1 hour 30 minutes

Ingredients

For the cake

- One cup of almond flour

- Three table spoons of coconut flavor
- A little water
- Half cup of soft butter (make the butter soft by placing at room temperature for some time)
- 2 eggs
- Two table spoons of protein powder

- One table spoon of vanilla extract
- One table spoon of baking powder
- Three table spoons of whipped cream
- A pinch of salt
- Four table spoons of granulated swerve sweetener

For the butter glaze

- Two table spoons of butter
- Half tablespoon of water
- A quarter cup of granulated swerve sweetener
- Half table spoon of vanilla essence

For the garnishing

- One table spoon of swerve sweetener

Preparation

For the cake

- Pre heat an oven to about 350F, get a cake baking pan, add a little butter to it and grease the pan with the butter, then put two table spoons of almond flour in the pan and dust it with the flour.
- Put the dry ingredients (the almond flour, the baking powder, the salt, the coconut flour and the protein powder) in a bowl and mix them together.
- Get another bowl and beat the swerve sweetener and the butter together until the mixture turns fluffy and very light. Add the vanilla extract and egg to the mixture and beat it together.
- Add the first mixture (the almond flour mixture) to the butter mixture and beat together. Then add the whipping cream and the water to the mixture and beat well until it combines very well.

- Pour the batter into the already greased and dusted baking pan. Bake it until it becomes firm and the color changes to a golden-brown color. This should take about an hour.

For the butter glaze

- Place a medium-sized saucepan on medium heat, put the butter and the swerve sweetener in the saucepan and let them melt together. Mix this mixture well to make it combine. Also add the vanilla extract and the water and whisk them well until the mixture is fully combined.
- Create holes in the cake in the baking pan. This can be done with a skewer.
- Pour the butter glaze on the cake in the baking pan while it is still warm and let the cake with the butter glaze get cooled down in the pan.
- Take away the cake from the baking pan and put it on a serving plate. Be careful to use a knife to make the sides of the cake get loosened so as to make the whole of the cake remove without any dents.
- While the cake is on the serving plate, use the powdered swerve sweetener to dust the top and the sides of the cake.
- The cake is ready to be served. You can serve with sweetened whipped cream and/or fresh strawberries.

20.   Texas Cheese Cake

It is not restricted to the Americans alone as the name implies. It is consumed all over the world and is a great dessert on the keto diet list.

Nutritional content

- Total Calories: 230 calories
- Calories from fat: 183 calories
- Fat: 20.3 g
- Carbohydrate: 5.9 g
- Protein: 5.8 g
- Fiber: 3.1 g

Serving Size: 4 servings

Preparation Time: 45 minutes

Ingredients

For the cake

- Half a cup of almond flour
- Two table spoons of coconut flour
- One table spoon of swerve sweetener
- Half table spoon of baking powder
- One table spoon of protein powder that is not flavored
- Three table spoons of salt
- A pinch of salt
- Two table spoons of water
- Two table spoons of whipping cream
- One egg
- Two table spoons of cocoa powder

For the frosting

- Two table spoons of pecans that are already chopped
- Two table spoons of butter
- A little water (about two tablespoons)
- Three table spoons of cocoa powder
- One heaped table spoon of whipping cream
- One tea spoon of vanilla extract
- Half a cup of swerve sweetener (in the powdered form)
- One tea spoon of xanthan gum

Preparation

For the cake

- First, heat the oven to about 325F before starting the preparation of the cake.
- Get a sheet pan (rimmed, about 10 by 15 inches), grease it with better.
- Mix the coconut flour, the almond flour, baking powder, sweetener, salt, and protein powder by whisking it in a mixing bowl. Do this till there is no lump in the mixture.
- Melt the cocoa powder and powder; add a little water till it is fully melted. Do this by putting the cocoa powder and butter in a small pot and place over a low heat. When

this melted mixture is boiling, remove it and pour it into the mixing bowl with the whisked dry ingredients.

- Add the vanilla extract, the eggs, a little water and cream. Stir them in until they have fully combined together
- Pour the batter in a baking pan and spread it in it.
- Place in the pre heated oven and bake it for about 20 minutes. By this time, the cake should be firm already.

For the frosting

- Put the cocoa powder, the butter, vanilla extract and a little water in a small sauce pan. Place it on medium heat and boil it till it simmers. Stir it to make it smooth. Add the vanilla extract and the sweetener (in powdered form) a little at a time and stir it while adding each portion. If there are any clumps in the mixture, stir and whisk it well to make the clumps dissolve.
- Add xanthan gum to the unclumped mixture and whisk it very well.
- Pour the frost on the cake while still warm and sprinkle pecans on the cake. Let the cake cool for about an hour (to make the frosting get set)
- Serve

21.   Cinnamon Roll Coffee Cake

This keto cake is filled with cinnamon and glazed with cream cheese that is sugar free. It is gluten free and also low in carbohydrate.

Nutritional Content In a serving

- Total calories: 222 calories
- Calories from fat: 174 calories
- Fat: 19.3 g
- Protein: 7.2 g
- Carbohydrate: 5.4 g

Serving size: 4 portions (a small sized cake)

Preparation time: 50 minutes

Ingredients

For the cake

- 1 cup of almond flour
- A quarter table spoon of already melted butter
- A quarter table spoon of almond milk
- A quarter cup of swerve sweetener
- Half table spoon of vanilla extract
- 1 egg
- A pinch of salt
- Two table spoons of protein powder that is unflavored
- A quarter table spoon of baking powder

For the cinnamon filling

- One table spoon of cinnamon in the ground form
- One table spoon of swerve sweetener in the powdered form

For the cream cheese frosting

- A quarter table spoon of vanilla extract
- A quarter table spoon of swerve sweetener
- One table spoon of cheese cream that is already softened
- A quarter table spoon of heavy whipping cream.

Preparation

- Get a small baking pan and grease it with butter
- Heat the oven to 325F
- Put the ground cinnamon in a small mixing bowl and add the swerve sweetener, then mix it very well. When it has mixed well enough, leave it and start to prepare the cake.
- Add all the dry ingredients for the cake in a large bowl. This includes the almond flour, the salt, the protein, the baking powder and sweetener. Mix them well by whisking them together.

- Add the already melted butter, the eggs, almond milk and vanilla extract and stir vigorously as you add the ingredients for easy and thorough combination.
- Put about a half of the batter into the greased baking pan and spread it. Then add more than half of the prepared cinnamon filling into the baking pan and add the remaining batter on top of the cinnamon filling. Spread it with a spatula.
- Bake until the top of the cake is golden brown in color. This should take about 35 minutes.
- Remove the cake into a serving plate and let it get cool.
- Add cream, cream cheese, vanilla extract, and the powdered erythritol into a bowl and mix in a small bowl to make the frosting. Beat the mixture well until it is well combined and smooth.
- Pipe the frosting on the cooled cake.

22.   Peanut Butter Mug Cake

It is important to work through the preparation of the peanut butter mug cake quickly because peanut butter thickens the cake batter the longer it waits.

Nutrition value of a serving (one mug cake)

- Total calories: 210 calories
- Calories from fat: 160 calories
- Fat: 17.8 g
- Protein: 6.4 g
- Fiber: 3 g

Serving size: 5 portions (5 mug cakes)   Preparation time: 5 minutes

Ingredients

- A quarter cup of peanut butter
- A quarter cup of butter
- Half cup of almond flour
- 3 table spoons of chocolate chips that are sugar free
- Half a table spoon of vanilla extract
- A quarter cup of swerve sweetener
- One table spoon of baking powder
- A little water

- Two eggs

Preparation

- Put the peanut butter and the butter in a bowl that is microwave save and place in the microwave to melt it. Make use the melted mixture is smooth.
- Put the almond flour, the sweetener and the baking powder in a bowl and mix together by whisking it. Add the peanut butter, melted, and butter mixture, the eggs, vanilla extract and a little water and stir it well till it combines. Also add the chocolate chips and stir it.
- Divide the batter into 5 mugs and bake in the microwave for about a minute each. It should be puff and set by this time.
- The cake can now be served. Ensure you serve it hot

23.   Ginger bread Cake Roll

Nutrition value of a serving

- Calories: 206 calories
- Calories from fat: 163 g
- Fat: 18.06 g
- Protein: 5.68 g
- Carbohydrate: 3.99g

Serving size: 4 servings   Preparation Time: 60 minutes

Ingredients

For the cake

- Half cup of almond flour
- One table spoon of ethical approval
- A quarter cup of a powdered sweetener
- Half tablespoon of grass-fed gelatin
- One eighth table spoon of cream of tarter
- A quarter table spoon of powdered ginger
- A pinch of salt
- A little cinnamon powder
- A quarter table spoon of vanilla extract

- One eight of powdered cloves
- One large egg

For the vanilla cream filling

- One cup of softened cream cheese
- Half cup of whipping cream
- Two table spoon of powdered sweetener
- A quarter tablespoon of vanilla extract

Preparation

For the cake

- Heat the oven to 350F before starting the cake preparation process. Place a parchment paper in a baking pan and line the baking pan with it. Use a little butter to grease the sides of the baking pan and also the parchment paper.
- Whisk the almond flour, the cocoa powder, the powdered sweetener, ginger, gelatin, powdered cloves together in a medium mixing bowl.
- Get another mixing bowl and mix the granulated sugar together with the egg yolk until the mixture gets thickened and the color turns light yellow.
- Also add the vanilla extract and beat the mixture well.
- Beat the egg whites and the cream of tartar and a little salt together in another mixing bowl until the mixture becomes frothy. When it is already frothy, add the remaining sweetener and beat it well.
- Fold the beat egg yolks into the beat egg whites gently. Then fold this into the almond flour mixture. Be careful not to make it deflated.
- Make the batter spread in to the already greased baking pan and bake for 12 minutes, until it springs back when the top is touched.
- Take it away from the oven and let it get cooled a little before removing it. You can to remove it by using a knife to make the edges loosen. Cover the cake with another piece of parchment paper and also use a kitchen towel to cover it. Put another baking sheet that is large on top of it and flip the cake over.

- Peel the parchment paper gently from the cake and also roll up the kitchen towel gently and let the cake cool down.

For the vanilla cream filling

- Beat half of the whipping cream with the cream cheese in a mixing bowl. Beat it till it becomes smooth.
- Beat the remaining whipping cream and the sweetener in a big mixing bowl. Then add the vanilla extract and the mixture of the whipping cream and beat very well, but do not over beat it. Keep about half of the mixture to decorate the cake.
- Unroll the cake carefully. Let the cake curl up on the ends and do not lay it down flat completely.
- Spread the rest of the filling on the cake and roll it up back gently. Do not roll it up back with the kitchen towel.
- Place it on a serving plate. Place the seam side down.
- Put the remaining cream mixture on the center of the cake in different shapes. You can use an icing pipe to achieve desired shapes.
- Keep In the refrigerator.

24.   Keto Pumpkin Cheese cake

Nutrition Value of a serving

- Total calories: 246 g
- Calories from fat: 211 g
- Fat: 23. 4 g

- Protein: 5.3 g
- Carbohydrates: 3.23 g
- Fiber: 1.1 g

Serving size: 4 servings

Preparation Time: 55 minutes + chill time

Ingredients

For the crust

- A quarter cup of almond flour
- Half table spoon of melted butter

- One table spoon of powdered sweetener
- A pinch of salt
- A quarter table spoon of powdered ginger
- A quarter table spoon of cinnamon powder

For the pumpkin cheese cake

- A cup of softened cheese
- One egg
- Half a cup of softened cream cheese
- Half table spoon of pumpkin pie spice
- Three table spoons of pumpkin puree
- Half tablespoon of vanilla extract

Preparation

For the crust

- Whisk the almond flour, the spices, salt and the sweetener together in a big mixing bowl. Add the butter that is now melted and stir until the mixture becomes clumpy.
- Pour the mixture into a spring form baking pan.

For the filing

- Beat the softened cheese and the cream cheese together until it combines well. Add the sweetener and stir well until it becomes smooth.
- Add the pumpkin pie spice, pumpkin puree, the vanilla extract and combine it well by beating it well. Add the egg and continue beating it until it combines well.
- Use a large foil paper to wrap the bottom of the spring form pan. Wrap it tightly. Put a paper towel over the pan. Be careful not to make it touch the cake. Then wrap another foil over the cake top. The reason for wrapping with foil is to prevent excess moisture from entering the cake.
- Bake the cake for about 30 minutes; bring it to cool it down.
- Refrigerate for about four hours. When it is chilled, use a knife to remove the cake.
- If you like, you can add a topping of caramel sauce and whipped cream

25.   Cannoli Sheet Cake

Nutrition value of a serving

- Total calories: 235 calories
- Calories from fat: 180 calories
- Fat: 20 g

- Protein: 6.8 g
- Carbohydrates: 6.2 g
- Calcium: 2.9 mg

Serving size: 5 servings

Preparation Time: 40 minutes

Ingredients

For the sheet cake

- Half cup of almond flour
- Half table spoon of vanilla extract
- A quarter cup of sweetener
- A little water
- Two table spoons of coconut flour

- Three table spoons of melted butter
- Two table spoons of protein powder
- One egg
- A pinch of salt
- Half table spoon of baking powder

For the cannoli cream frosting

- A quarter cup of milk ricotta
- Two tablespoons of chocolate chips (sugar free)
- Two table spoon of softened cheese cream
- A quarter table spoon of vanilla extract
- A quarter cup of powdered sweetener
- A quarter cup of heavy whipping cream

Preparation

- Heat the oven to about 325F. Grease a small jelly roll pan to avoid the cake sticking to the bottom of the pan.
- Whisk the almond flour, coconut flour, sweetener, protein powder, baking powder, and the salt in a big mixing bowl. Add the, already melted butter, eggs, water, and the vanilla extract and stir until they have combined very well.

- The batter is then poured into the already prepared baking pan and spread it so that there is an even distribution of the batter in the baking pan. Bake the bake for about 22 minutes till the color becomes golden brown and becomes firm while touched.
- Remove the baking pan from the oven and let cool completely.

26.   Coconut Flour Chocolate Cupcake

Nutritional Value of a serving

Total Calories: 268 calories

Calories from fat:

Serving Size: 4 servings (4 cup cakes)

Preparation Time: 35 minutes

Ingredients

- Four table spoons of melted butter
- Three table spoon of cocoa butter
- Three table spoons of almond cream that is unsweetened
- Two eggs
- A pinch of salt
- Three table spoons of sweetener
- One table spoon of baking powder
- One table spoon of vanilla essence

For the butter cream

- Half cup of sweetener
- One table spoon of instant coffee
- Two table spoons of softened cream cheese
- A little hot water
- Half a cup of whipping cream

Preparation

For the cup cakes

- Heat the oven to 370 F
- Use some parchment paper to line the insides of the muffin tin

- Add the cocoa powder, melted butter, the espresso powder and melted butter together in a big mixing bowl and whisk them together.
- Add the vanilla essence and eggs to the mixture then add the baking powder, coconut flour, a pinch of salt and the sweetener, and then beat well to combine it together.

27.   Classic New York Keto Cheese Cake

Nutritional Value of a serving

- Total calories: 284 calories
- Calories from fat; 222 calories
- Fat: 24.7 gram

- Carbohydrate: 2.9 grams
- Protein; 5.3 grams

Serving Size: 4 servings

Preparation Time: 1 hour 45 minutes + 4 hours of chill

Ingredients

- 4 table spoons of cream cheese that is already softened
- One table spoon of vanilla extract
- One egg
- Two table spoons of soft butter that is not salted
- One table spoon of lemon zest that is grated
- Five table spoons of powdered sweetener
- Three table spoons of sour cream that is at room temperature

Preparation

- Get the oven pre heated to about 300F. Get a spring form pan and grease it with butter. Grease it well so that the cake would remove well.
- Put a parchment paper that is already cut to the shape of the spring form pan in the bottom of the pan. Grease the parchment paper with butter. Wrap he outside of the pan with aluminum foil paper to cover the bottom of the pan and also to cover the outside of the pan more than half way up.

- Get a mixing bowl and add the cream cheese and butter and beat it till it becomes smooth. Also add the sweetener and beat till the mixture has combined very well. Add the egg into the mixture and beat again.
- Put the lemon zest, sour cream and also the vanilla extract and beat it until it is very smooth and it has fully combined. Pour the batter into the already greased spring form pan and smoothen the top of the batter.
- Put the spring form pan in a big roasting pan so that the sides don't touch. Put the roasting pan in the oven. Pour some boiling water carefully into the roasting pan until it reaches half of the sides.
- Bake for about 90 minutes and let it cool after baking.
- When it is cool, carefully remove the cake and refrigerate for 4 hours before serving.

28.   Triple Chocolate Mousse Cake

Nutritional Value of a Serving

- Total calories: 293 calories
- Calories from fat: 233 calories
- Fat: 25. 94 g
- Protein: 6.32 g
- Carbohydrates: 6. 03g
- Cholesterol: 108 mg
- Fiber: 2.55g

Serving Size: 1 serving (a big size cake)   Preparation Time: 3 hours 45 minutes

Ingredients

For the cake

- A cup of almond flour
- Three table spoons of coconut flour
- Half of a small cup of water
- A pinch of salt
- Three table spoons of cocoa powder
- One table spoon of vanilla extract
- Three table spoons of protein powder
- Two big eggs

- Two table spoons of baking powder
- Ten table spoons of butter
- Half cup of sweetener
- One tablespoon of coffee granules

For the Mousse Layers

- Double recipe white chocolate mousse
- One recipe blender chocolate mousse
- A quarter table spoon of xanthan gum

Preparation

For the cake

- Get the oven heated to 325F before starting the preparation of the cake.
- Grease a spring form baking pan well
- Get a medium mixing bowl, add the coconut flour, almond flour, cocoa powder, and protein powder, and baking powder, salt and instant coffee and whisk them together.
- Get a large mixing bowl and beat the sweetener and the butter until they have combined very well. Add the vanilla extract, the eggs and water and beat it well. Also add the almond flour mixture and beat well.
- Pour the batter into the already greased spring form pan and smoothen it. Bake the cake for about 30 minutes. It should be firm to the touch by this time. Remove the pan from the oven and let it get cool.

For the chocolate mousse layers

- Mix the chocolate mousse together and pour the mixture on top of the already cooled cake in the pan and chill for an hour.
- Before you lose the sides of the spring form pan, use a knife (sharp) to loosen the cake from the sides.
- Remove the cake and cut into slices and serve.

CANDY AND CONFECTION

29.   High Protein green Gummies

Preparation time: 11 minutes

Ingredients

- Half a cup of collagelatin
- One and a half cups of green juice (mixture of lemon, basil, lime, celery, spinach and cucumber)
- Two table spoons of sweetener

Preparation

- Mix the green juice and collagelatin together and let it thicken.
- When it has thickened, heat in a sauce pan on low heat until the gelatin is dissolved completely.
- Pour the mixture into the gum molds and place in the freezer.
- When they are still, remove and serve.

30.   Dark Chocolate with Matcha Coconut Butter Keto cups

Serving Size: 3 big cups   Preparation Time: 10 minutes

Ingredients

For the dark chocolate

- 3 table spoons of hundred percent dark chocolate bar
- One table spoon of coconut oil

For the Matcha coconut butter filling

- Half table spoon of organic Matcha powder
- Half table spoon of coconut milk
- A quarter cup of coconut butter
- A quarter table spoon of vanilla extract

Preparation

- Get a big muffin tin and line it with parchment paper.
- Chop the chocolate bar. Heat the coconut oil and chocolate till they melt together.

- Add a tablespoon of the melted chocolate to every of the lined muffin tins and use a spoon to push the chocolate to about a quarter of the sides. Freeze for 10 minutes.
- Add all the ingredients for the Matcha filling into a blender and blend until it has combined really well.
- Remove the pan from the freezer and add the Matcha filling in the center of the chocolate cups. Freeze again and serve.

31.   Chocolate Covered Bacon

Nutritional Value of a serving

- Calories: 370
- Fat: 28g
- Protein: 15g
- Carbohydrates: 11g
- Fiber: 3g

- Total Sugars: 0g
- Sugar Alcohols: 4.5g
- Net Carbs: 3.5g
- Sodium: 380mg

Serving size: 2 servings

Preparation Time: 20 minutes

Ingredients

- 4 slices of organic pastured bacon
- Half of a melted chocolate bar
- A pinch of salt

Preparation

- Preheat the oven to 350F and line a baking tray with baking paper.
- When the oven is hot, place the bacon pieces onto the lined tray evenly.
- Place the tray in the oven to cook and make sure you keep an eye on the bacon and check it every 5-10 minutes until you reach your desired crispiness.
- When the bacon is ready, remove it from the oven and carefully drain away the excess fat into a glass jar. Pat the bacon slices with a paper towel if there is still excess fat.

- Pour the melted chocolate into a small cup or glass jar and begin to dip the bacon into the melted chocolate so they're half covered.

- You can eat it straight away like this, or if you prefer, you can also place the chocolate coated bacon onto a plate lined with baking paper and repeat the process for the rest of the bacon.

- Once all the bacon pieces are covered in chocolate, place them in the fridge and allow the chocolate to harden.

- Remove from fridge when it is ready and serve

32.   Low Carb almond Joy Bon Buns

Nutritional value of a serving

- Calories – 198
- Fat – 18 g
- Carbohydrates – 7 g
- Protein – 3 g

Preparation time – 30 minutes

Serving size – 12 bonbons

Ingredients

- Half cup of sweetened condensed milk
- One cup of shredded coconut that is unsweetened
- Two table spoons of coconut oil
- One cup of chocolate chips
- Half cup of almond that is sliced

Preparation

- Mix all the ingredients together.
- Form the mixture into balls and place on a baking sheet then put in the freezer
- When it is hardened, serve.

33.   Zucchini Chips

The zucchini is a squash plant which can reach nearly 1 m in length, but is usually harvested when still immature at about 15 to 25 cm. A zucchini is a thin-skinned cultivar of what in Britain and Ireland is referred to as a marrow.

Nutritional content in a serving

Calories: 15.2 calories   Sodium: 77.3mg   Carbohydrate: 3.

Fat: 0.1 gram   Potassium: 227.7mg

Cholesterol: 0 gram   Protein: 0.6g

Portion: 4 servings   Preparation Time; 1hr 40 minutes

Ingredients

- Cooking spray
- Two zucchinis, sliced very thinly into coins
- One tablespoon of extra-virgin olive oil for oven version only
- One tablespoon of seasoning
- One tablespoon of dried oregano
- Kosher salt
- Freshly ground black pepper

Utensils/Equipment

- Oven/air fryer
- Knife
- Large bowl

Preparation

Oven Version

- Pre heat the oven to about 230 degree Celsius.

- Put cooking spray on a big baking sheet and grease it with it.
- Slice all the zucchini very thin and also make sure that the excess water is removed.
- Add the zucchini in a big bowl; add a little oil, every of the seasonings, salt and pepper.
- Put the mixture on a baking sheet
- Bake it till when it is crispy
- Let it cool. Serve when it is cool

Air Fryer

- Put some cooking spray on the air fryer and grease the air fryer with it.
- Slice all the zucchini very thin. Be sure that the excess water in the sliced zucchini is removed.
- Place the zucchini in a big bowl; add a little oil, seasonings, salt and paper.
- Put the mixture in the air fryer
- Airs fry it for about 380 degree Celsius for about six minutes.
- Flip it over and cook it for another seven minutes.
- Remove the chips when they are golden in color and crispy
- Allow to cool a little, then serve

34.   Low Carb Chocolate

Nutritional value of a serving (a bar)
- Total Calories: 216

Serving Size: 12 bars   Preparation Time: 40 minutes

Ingredients

For the coconut layer (bottom)
- Two cups of shredded coconut that is unsweetened
- One table spoon of sweetener
- Half cup of melted coconut oil

For the chocolate topping layer
- One table spoon of coconut oil

- Two table spoons of granulated sweetener
- One cup of unsweetened chocolate

Preparation

For the coconut layer

- Add all the ingredients for the coconut layer into a food processor and process until the mixture is well combined.
- Press the combined mixture into the bottom of a silicon pan and refrigerate while the topping is being prepared.

For the Chocolate Layer

- Melt the coconut and chocolate together in a microwave. Add the sweetener and stir.
- Spread this chocolate layer on the coconut layer evenly and freeze for 30 minutes.
- Remove and cut into bars and serve.

35.   Coconut Oil Candies

Ingredients

- One cup of cold pressed coconut oil
- Two table spoons of almond butter
- Two table spoons of cocoa powder that is not sweetener
- Two tablespoons of powdered sweetener
- One tablespoon of vanilla extract
- A pinch of salt

Preparation

- Put all the ingredients in a mixing bowl and mix until it is smooth,
- Pour into parchment papers and wrap.
- Refrigerate until they are hard and solid.

36. Sugar Free Chocolate Bark with Bacon and Almonds

Nutritional value

- Calories – 157
- Fat – 12.8 g
- Protein – 4 g
- Fiber – 7.5 g

Serving Size – 8   Preparation Time - 30 minutes

Ingredients

- 2 slices of already cooked and crumbled bacon
- Half a cup of almonds that are chopped already
- Two cups of chocolate chips

Preparation

- Melt the chocolate chips.
- Add all the ingredients and stir well
- Pour the mixture into a baking sheet. Sprinkle in the cooked bacon that are already crumbled into the chocolate.
- Freeze until it is very hard and peel away the parchment paper, then break it into pieces and serve.

37. Keto White Chocolate

Preparation Time – 10 minutes + 3 hours for chill

Ingredients

- Three table spoons of Cocoa butter
- 5 table spoons of powdered sweetener
- Toppings of choice

Preparation

- Line a baking sheet with parchment paper
- Melt the cocoa butter and add the sweetener, whisk it well until it has combined well.

- Pour the mixture into the lined baking sheet and freeze for 3 hours.

FROZEN DESSERTS

38.   Low Carb Vanilla Bean Ice Cream

Serving Size: 4 servings   Preparation Time: 40 minutes

Ingredients
- A quarter cup of sweetener
- A pinch of salt
- A quarter table spoon of xanthan gum
- Half table spoon of vanilla extract
- One halved vanilla bean
- Half cup of vanilla almond milk hat is unsweetened
- One egg
- One cup of whipping cream

Preparation
- Mix all the ingredients until they are fully combined
- Pour the mixture into the ice cream maker and process until it is thick and becomes frozen.

39.   Keto Avocado Popsicles

Nutritional value of a serving
- Calories – 33
- Protein – 1 g
- Fat – 3 g

Preparation Time: 30 minutes

Ingredients

- One avocado
- One table spoon of cocoa butter
- Three table spoons of sweetener
- One table spoon of lemon juice
- One cup of chocolate (low carb)
- One cup of unsweetened almond milk

Preparation

- Mix all the ingredients until they are fully combined
- Pour the mixture into the ice cream maker and process until it is thick and becomes frozen.

40.   Keto Chocolate Ice Cream

Ingredients

- Powdered sweetener
- Heavy cream
- Eggs
- Powdered cocoa
- Vanilla extract

Preparation

- Mix all the ingredients until they are fully combined
- Pour the mixture into the ice cream maker and process until it is thick and becomes frozen.

41.   Keto Strawberry Ice cream

Ingredients

- Powdered sweetener
- Heavy cream
- Eggs
- Powdered strawberry
- Vanilla extract

Preparation

- Mix all the ingredients until they are fully combined
- Pour the mixture into the ice cream maker and process until it is thick and becomes frozen.

42.   Magical Frozen Fudge Pops

Ingredients

- Powdered sweetener
- Heavy cream
- Eggs
- Powdered strawberry or any other base of desired flavor
- Vanilla extract

Preparation

- Mix all the ingredients until they are fully combined
- Pour the mixture into the ice cream maker and process until it is thick and becomes frozen.

43.   No Churn Mint Chocolate Chip Ice Cream

Serving size – 3 servings

Preparation time – 30 minutes

Ingredients

- One table spoon mint leaves
- One table spoon Powdered sweetener
- One table spoon Heavy cream
- One Eggs
- One table spoon of chocolate chips
- Vanilla extract to taste

Preparation

- Mix all the ingredients until they are fully combined
- Pour the mixture into the ice cream maker and process until it is thick and becomes frozen.

44.   Chocolate Cookie Dough Keto Ice cream

Serving size – 3 servings

Preparation time – 30 minutes

Ingredients

- One table spoon of chocolate cookies
- One table spoon Powdered sweetener
- One table spoon Heavy cream
- One Eggs
- One table spoon of chocolate chips
- Vanilla extract to taste
- One chocolate bar

Preparation

- Mix all the ingredients until they are fully combined
- Pour the mixture into the ice cream maker and process until it is thick and becomes frozen

45.   Raspberry Lemon Keto Ice Cream

Serving size – 3 servings

Preparation time – 30 minutes

Ingredients

- One table spoon of raspberry powder
- One table spoon Powdered sweetener
- One table spoon Heavy cream
- One Eggs
- One table spoon of lemon juice
- Vanilla extract to taste

Preparation

- Mix all the ingredients until they are fully combined
- Pour the mixture into the ice cream maker and process until it is thick and becomes frozen

46.   Keto Pumpkin Ice cream

Serving size – 3 servings

Preparation time – 30 minutes

Ingredients

- One table spoon of pumpkin puree
- One table spoon Powdered sweetener
- One table spoon Heavy cream
- One Egg
- Vanilla extract to taste

Preparation

- Mix all the ingredients until they are fully combined
- The mixture is then poured into the ice cream maker and process until it is thick and becomes frozen

47.   Keto Orange Chocolate Ice Cream

Serving size – 3 servings

Preparation time – 30 minutes

Ingredients

- One table spoon of chocolate chips
- One table spoon Powdered sweetener
- Half cup of orange juice
- One table spoon Heavy cream
- One Egg
- Vanilla extract to taste

Preparation

- All the ingredients are mixed till until they are fully combined

The mixture is then poured into the ice cream maker and process until it is thick and becomes frozen.

48.   Keto Mango Chocolate Ice Cream

Serving size – 3 servings
Preparation time – 30 minutes
Ingredients

- One table spoon of chocolate chips
- One table spoon Powdered sweetener
- Half cup of mango juice
- One table spoon Heavy cream
- One Egg
- Vanilla extract to taste

Preparation

- All the ingredients are mixed till they are well mixed.

The mixture is then poured into the ice cream maker and process until it is thick and becomes frozen.

49.   Keto Orange Vanilla Ice Cream

Serving size – 3 servings
Preparation time – 30 minutes
Ingredients

- One table spoon of vanilla powder

- One table spoon Powdered sweetener
- Half cup of orange juice
- One table spoon Heavy cream
- One Egg
- Vanilla extract to taste

Preparation

- The ingredients are all mixed until fully combined.
- The mixture is then poured into the ice cream maker and process until it is thick and becomes frozen.

50.   Keto Lemon Strawberry Ice Cream

Serving size – 3 servings

Preparation time – 30 minutes

Ingredients

- One table spoon of strawberry flavor
- One table spoon Powdered sweetener
- Half cup of lemon juice
- One table spoon Heavy cream
- One Egg

Preparation

- The ingredients are mixed until fully combined.
- The mixture is then poured into the ice cream maker and process until it is thick and becomes frozen.

CUSTARD AND MOUSSE

51.   Keto Pots de Crème

Preparation time – 1 hour

Serving size – 6 servings

Ingredients

- Four egg yolks
- Three table spoons of heavy cream
- A pinch of salt
- One table spoon of vanilla extract
- Three table spoons of chocolate chips
- Three table spoons of sweetener

Preparation

- Melt the chocolate chips, the heavy cream together and add the sweetener and salt.
- Put the egg yolks in the mixture making sure to whisk it as each yolk is added.
- Pour the mixture into mason jars and seal them. Put the jars in a water bath at 176F and cook for an hour.
- Remove the jars and cool in the fridge.
- Serve

52.   CHIA SEED PUDDING

Chia is a generally healthy food. It contains high fiber (which helps with bowel movement and also helps in weight loss). It also contains omega 3 fatty acid which is very useful in fighting inflammation). It is gluten free and also a ketogenic diet. It is also very easy and not stressful to prepare. The preparation takes just five minutes.

Nutritional Content in one serving (a cup of Chia seed pudding)

Calorie: 137 calories	Fat: omega 3:5 grams
Protein: 4 grams	Others: 4 grams
Fiber: 11 grams	Carbohydrate: 1 gram

It also has significant amounts of magnesium(about 50% of the recommended daily intake), Phosphorus (about 27% of the recommended intake daily), manganese (about 30% of the recommended intake daily), Calcium(about 18% of the recommended intake daily) and also some significant amounts of Potassium, Thiamine(Vitamin B1), Vitamin b2, Niacin(Vitamin B3) and Zinc.

Portion size: 4 servings

Preparation Time: 5 minutes (minus refrigeration time)

Utensils/ Equipment used

- A jar with lid
- Big spoon to stir
- Refrigerator

Ingredients

- Two cups of Chia seeds
- Six cups of dairy free milk of choice (Almond milk or Coconut milk could be used)
- Eight tablespoons of honey
- One tablespoon of vanilla flavor (or any other flavor of choice)

For the toppings, toppings of choice should be used (can be oranges, fresh berries, nuts)

Preparation

Use a Jar with lid

- Add the chia seeds, the honey, the milk and the vanilla flavor (or flavor of choice) to the jar.

- Cover with the lid and shake the jar well so as to make all the mixture to combine well.
- When the mixture is combined well, let the covered jar sit for about five minutes, stir it well again to let any other clumps in the mixture break up.
- Cover the jar and put the mixture into the fridge overnight.
- The pudding should not be liquidly, it should be thick. If it is not thick yet, add extra chia seeds (probably about half of a cup or till it is thick), stir well again to break up any clumps an refrigerate for another thirty minutes.
- As an alternate to these steps, you can just pep the pudding overnight and refrigerate overnight too.
- When pudding is ready, top it with toppings of choice (cherries, berries or nuts)

Pudding can be stored for about seven days in an airtight container

53.   Key Lime Pudding

Serving size – 6 servings   Preparation time – 1 hour

Ingredients
- Four egg yolks
- Three table spoons of heavy cream
- A pinch of salt
- One table spoon of vanilla extract
- Three table spoons of lime juice
- Three table spoons of sweetener

Preparation
- The ingredients minus the egg yolks are added together and mixed well.
- Put the egg yolks in the mixture making sure to whisk it as each yolk is added.
- Pour the mixture into mason jars and seal them. Put the jars in a water bath at 176F and cook for an hour.
- Remove the jars and cool in the fridge.

- Serve

54.   Low Carb Coconut Pudding

Total Calories – 242 kcal   Serving size – 6 servings   Preparation time – 1 hour

Ingredients
- Three cups of coconut milk
- Three table spoons of gelatin
- A pinch of salt
- One table spoon of vanilla extract

- Three tablespoons of coconut sweetener

Preparation
- Boil the coconut milk in a sauce pan and stir to prevent lumping.
- Add the gelatin and allow it to get thickened.
- Add the remaining ingredients and boil for 10 minutes, then pour into jars and refrigerate overnight.
- Serve

55.   Keto Chocolate Mousse

Preparation time – 10 minutes   Serving size – 4 servings
                                       Total calories – 218 kcal

Ingredients
- One cup of whipping cream
- A pinch of salt
- Half cup of powdered sweetener
- A quarter cup of cocoa powder
- One table spoon of vanilla extract

Preparation

- Mix all the ingredients together till they are fully combined and serve

56. Cold Brew Mocha Coffee Panna Cotta

Total Calories – 242 kcal   Serving size – 6 servings   Preparation time – 1 hour

Ingredients

- Three cups of coconut milk
- Three table spoons of gelatin
- A pinch of salt
- One table spoon of vanilla extract

- Three tablespoons of coconut sweetener

Preparation

- Boil the coconut milk in a sauce pan and stir to prevent lumping.
- Add the gelatin and allow it to get thickened.
- Add the remaining ingredients and boil for 10 minutes then pour into jars and refrigerate overnight.
- Serve

57. Coconut Strawberry Mousse

Preparation time – 10 minutes   Serving size – 4 servings
Total calories – 223 kcal

Ingredients

- One cup of coconut milk
- A pinch of salt
- Half cup of powdered sweetener

- A quarter cup of strawberry powder
- One table spoon of vanilla extract

Preparation

- Mix all the ingredients together until they are fully combined and serve.

58.   Smoky onion jam squash

For the Onion Jam

- One tablespoon of butter
- Three sprigs of fan
- Half cup of red wine vinegar
- A quarter cup of maple syrup
- One tablespoon of olive oil
- One thinly sliced large onions
- A Pinch of salt
- A Pinch of chili flakes
- One teaspoon of smoked paprika

59.   For the Roasted Squash

- One big squash (cut into halves and seeded)
- Chili flake
- Two tablespoons of Olive oil
- Sea salt

Preparation

For the onion jam:

- Get a large skillet. Set it over a moderately high heat. Then add the onions, butter, a little olive oil and a pinch of salt.
- Add the sprigs of the chili thyme and chili flakes, and then stir well.

- Cook the onions till they start to get soft and also start to turn brown. When the onions start to turn brown and crisp, turn the heat down so as aid caramelization of the sugars present in the onions.
- Once the onions turn fine brown color, add the vinegar and maple syrup, make sure to stir it in.
- Then cook for about ten minutes.
- Turn off the heat and wait for it to cool a little.
- Pluck off the thyme sprigs from the jam.
- Roast the squash as the jam cools.

60.   Keto vanilla chocolate mousse

Preparation time – 10 minutes

Serving size – 4 servings
Total calories – 218 kcal

Ingredients
- One cup of whipping cream
- A pinch of salt
- Half cup of powdered sweetener
- A quarter cup of cocoa powder
- One table spoon of vanilla extract

Preparation
- Mix all the ingredients till they are fully combines and serve.

61.   Keto pumpkin chocolate Mousse

Preparation time – 10 minutes

Serving size – 4 servings

Total calories – 296 kcal

Ingredients

- Three table spoons of pumpkin puree
- One cup of whipping cream
- A pinch of salt
- Half cup of powdered sweetener
- A quarter cup of cocoa powder
- One table spoon of vanilla extract

Preparation

- Mix all the ingredients till they are fully combines and serve.

PIES AND TARTS

62.   Mahi-Mahi fillet with lemon-garlic dressing

Ingredients:

- Butter: 3 tbsp.
- Olive oil: 1 tbsp.
- Mahi-Mahi Fillet: 500 g.
- Cloves finely chopped: 3
- Garlic to taste
- Juice and zest of one lemon
- Parsley, finely chopped: 3 tbsp.

Preparation

- In a large pan, heat 1 tbsp. l butter and add the olive, Salt, pepper
- Put the Mahi-Mahi fillet on a pan. Fry your fish properly for about 3-4 minutes on each side until it turns golden.
- After putting the fillet on a plate, melt the remaining 2 tbsp in a pan. l butter, add garlic and fry for 1-2 minutes.
- Add garlic lemon zest, juice and parsley. Stir and remove the sauce from the heat.
- Put the finished sauce on the fish fillet. Garnish the finished dish with lemon slices if desired.

63.   Crispy Cauliflower Bites

They have an appetizing crunch and they are low in sugar, spicy and free of gluten.

Portion Size: 6 servings

Preparation time: 40 minutes

Ingredients

- One head of cauliflower (cut in to florets.)
- Half tablespoon of garlic powder.

- Half tablespoon of seasoning.
- one cup of breadcrumbs (gluten free)
- Half cup of aquafaba.

Utensils/equipment

- Oven
- Bowl
- Spoon
- Pot
- Baking pan

Preparation

- Preheat the oven to 450 degrees F.
- Add the garlic powder and also the season to the cauliflower to season it.
- Dip the cauliflower in the aquafaba and shake it to remove the excess.
- Coat the cauliflower dipped in the aquafaba with the breadcrumbs and shake the excess off.
- Place it on a baking pan lined with parchment paper.
- Bake it for fifteen minutes.
- For the florets to bake evenly throughout, flip it over.
- Bake for another 15 minutes.
- Serve immediately.

Note

- Different seasonings of choice can be used to make different exciting flavors.

64. Keto Chocolate Tart

Serving size – 8 servings

Preparation Time – 2 hours

Ingredients

CRUST

- 6 tbsp of Coconut flour
- 2 tbsp of sweetener
- 4 tbsp of melted butter
- 1 large egg

FILLING

- oz Unsweetened Bakers Chocolate
- 1/2 cup Heavy Whipping Cream
- 1/4 cup of powdered sweetener
- 1 large Egg
- 1 oz Cream Cheese
- 20 drops of liquid sweetener

Preparation

- Before starting, heat the oven to a temperature of about 350 degrees.
- Combine all the ingredients for the crust in a small bowl for mixing.
- Split the crust mixture into two equal halves using two 4-inch pans.
- Use your hands or spatula to push the crust mixture towards the sides of the pan.
- Puncture some holes in the crust and let it bake for up to 12 minutes. While it is cooling, go ahead to make the filling.

65. Bacon Zucchini Boats

This keto diet is a very low-calorie (about 17 kcal per 100 g) product, and therefore it is recommended to add it to the diet with any diet. It contains vitamins A and C, carotene, as well as rich in potassium. These Low-carb diets are known to inevitably lead to digestive problems, but zucchini helps speed up metabolism and normalize metabolism.

Ingredients:

- Zucchini medium, cut in half: 3 pieces.
- Soft cream cheese: 220 g
- Artichokes finely chopped: 1/2 tbsp.
- Chopped spinach: 1/2 tbsp.
- Mozzarella grated: 1 tbsp.
- Grated Parmesan: 1/2 tbsp.
- Garlic, finely chopped: 1 clove
- Red pepper: 1/2 tsp
- Salt and pepper to taste
- Bacon: 12 slices

Preparation:
- Set the oven to 180 degrees. Prepare a baking rack by covering it with parchment paper.
- Remove the seeds from the zucchini halves.
- In a large bowl, combine cream, artichokes, spinach, mozzarella, parmesan, garlic, salt, black and red pepper.
- Put the cheese mixture in the boats. Wrap each in two slices of bacon and transfer to a wire rack.
- Bake the boats for about 40 minutes until the zucchini is soft and the bacon is crispy.

66.   Keto Berry Cobber - Mexican Stuffed Avocado

A low-carb, high-fat diet is simply impossible to imagine without an avocado. This product is oversaturated with healthy fats, vitamins and minerals, without which both a healthy diet and diets would be inferior.

Ingredients:

- Avocados cut in half with seeds removed: 4
- Lime juice:1 pc
- Olive oil: 1 tbsp
- Onion, finely chopped: 1 pc.
- Ground Beef: 450 g
- Spices tacos (mix): 30 g.
- Salt, pepper: to taste
- Mexican cheese Cotija grated: 2/3 tbsp.
- Lettuce, torn into small pieces: 1/2 tbsp.
- Cherry tomatoes cut into circles: 1/2 tbsp.
- Sour cream to taste

Preparation:

- Using a spoon, remove a little pulp from the avocado halves and transfer to a separate bowl. To prevent the flesh of the avocado from darkening, pour it with lime juice.
- Heat oil in a pan, fry onions, add minced meat and tacos, mix, season with salt and pepper and cook for 6-8 minutes until the meat turns pink. Transfer the minced meat from the pan to a separate bowl and get rid of excess fat.
- Fill each half of the avocado with meat, and then put the flesh of avocado, cheese, lettuce, cherry and sour cream.

67.   Lemon Coconut Custard Pie - Veggie Coconut wraps

They are a healthier alternative to tortillas or bread because they're low in carbohydrate and gluten free. Because coconut is rich in fiber, minerals and vitamins and coconut is the major ingredient in it, Coconut warps are also rich in fiber, minerals and vitamins.

Portion size: 4 wraps.   Preparation Time: 5 minutes

Ingredients

- Five wraps of coconut.
- Eight Tablespoons of green curry past.
- One thinly sliced red bell pepper.
- One sliced ripe avocado
- Three cups of chopped kale.
- Two cups of shredded carrots.
- One cup of fresh cilantro.
- Half cup of hummus.

Preparation

- Lay a coconut wrap on a clean cutting board.
- Mix the curry paste and hummus together.
- Spread the mix on the end of the wrap closet to you.
- Add the avocado, bell pepper, cilantro, kale and carrot and roll it tightly.
- Place it down on a serving platter (place the seam side down)
- Repeat for the remaining four coconut wraps.
- Serve immediately while fresh.

68.   Autumn-winter classic

Preparation time: 25mins   Serving size: 5 servings

Ingredients

- Almond flour: 190g
- Cinnamon: 1 tbsp. a spoon
- Ground ginger: 1 teaspoon
- Ground cloves: 1/4 teaspoon
- Ground Nutmeg: 1/4 teaspoon
- Baking powder: 1/2 tsp
- Butter: 50 g
- Sweetener: 30 g
- Egg: 1 pc

Preparation

- Get a medium sized bowl, combine almond flour, cinnamon, ginger, cloves, nutmeg, and baking powder. In a large bowl,
- Beat the sweetener, and then add the egg and flavor, beat, then add the dry ingredients and mix thoroughly.
- Form the dough into a ball and refrigerate for at least 30 minutes.
- Put your dough between two sides of the flour and roll it to a thickness of 0.5 cm.
- Cut out the shapes of the cookies and transfer them to a baking sheet. Send to the oven preheated to 180 ° C for 10-15 minutes, until golden brown

69.   Coconut Oil Candies

Ingredients

- One cup of cold pressed coconut oil
- Two table spoons of almond butter
- Two table spoons of cocoa powder that is not sweetener
- Two tablespoons of powdered sweetener
- One table spoon of vanilla extract

- A pinch of salt

Preparation

- Put all the ingredients into a mixing bowl and mix until it is smooth,
- Pour into parchment papers and wrap.
- Refrigerate until they are hard and solid.

70.   Classic New York Keto Cheese

Nutritional Value of a serving

- Total calories: 284 calories
- Calories from fat; 222 calories
- Fat: 24.7 gram
- Carbohydrate: 2.9 grams
- Protein; 5.3 grams

Serving Size: 4 servings

Preparation Time: 1 hour 45 minutes + 4 hours of chill

Ingredients

- 4 table spoons of cream cheese that is already softened
- One table spoon of vanilla extract
- One egg
- Two table spoons of soft butter that is not salted
- One table spoon of lemon zest that is grated
- Five table spoons of powdered sweetener
- Three table spoons of sour cream that is at room temperature

Preparation

- Get the oven pre heated to about 300F. Get a spring form pan and grease it with butter. Grease it well so that the cake would remove well.
- Put a parchment paper that is already cut to the shape of the spring form pan in the bottom of the pan. Grease the parchment paper with butter. Wrap he outside of the

pan with aluminum foil paper to cover the bottom of the pan and also to cover the outside of the pan more than half way up.

- Get a mixing bowl and add the cream cheese and butter and beat it till it becomes smooth. Also add the sweetener and beat till the mixture has combined very well. Add the egg into the mixture and beat again.
- Put the lemon zest, sour cream and also the vanilla extract and beat it until it is very smooth and it has fully combined. Pour the batter into the already greased spring form pan and smoothen the top of the batter.
- Put the spring form pan in a big roasting pan so that the sides don't touch. Put the roasting pan in the oven. Pour some boiling water carefully into the roasting pan until it reaches half of the sides.
- Bake for about 90 minutes and let it cool after baking.

When it is cool, carefully remove the cake and refrigerate for 4 hours before serving

BROWNIES

71.   Super Fudgy Cocoa Brownies

Total calories – 102 kcal

Preparation time – 35 minutes   Serving size – 4 servings

Ingredients

- Three table spoons of cocoa powder
- Half cup of almond flour
- A pinch of salt
- Two tablespoons of butter
- One egg
- Two table spoons of sweetener

Preparation

- Combine, in the right proportions, all the ingredients together and whisk well
- Pour into a baking pan and bake in the oven for about 20 minutes
- Allow to cool and cut into desired size

72.   Coconut Blondies

Preparation time – 35 minutes   Serving size – 4 servings

Ingredients

- Three table spoons of shredded coconut
- Half cup of coconut flour
- A pinch of salt
- Two table spoons of butter
- One egg
- Two table spoons of sweetener

Preparation

- Combine all the ingredients together and whisk well
- Pour into a baking pan and bake in the oven for about 20 minutes
- Allow to cool and cut into desired size

73.   Vanilla coconut brownies

Preparation time – 35 minutes   Serving size – 4 servings

Ingredients

- Three tablespoons of vanilla powder
- Half cup of coconut flour
- A pinch of salt
- Two tablespoons of butter
- One egg
- Two table spoons of sweetener

Preparation

- Combine all the ingredients together and whisk well
- Pour into a baking pan and bake in the oven for about 20 minutes
- Allow to cool and cut into desired size

74.   Chocolate coconut brownies

Preparation time – 35 minutes   Serving size – 4 servings

Ingredients

- Three table spoons of cocoa powder
- Half cup of coconut flour
- A pinch of salt
- Two table spoons of butter
- One egg
- Two table spoons of sweetener

Preparation

- Combine all the ingredients together and whisk well
- Pour into a baking pan and bake in the oven for about 20 minutes
- Allow to cool and cut into desired size

COOKIES

75.   Keto Protein Chocolate Chip Cookies

Ingredients

- one cup of almond nut
- 3 tbsp. grass-fed butter
- 3 table spoons of protein
- Sweetener to taste
- One table spoon apple cider vinegar
- A pinch of salt
-
- 2 table spoons of vanilla
- 1 egg
- Half table spoon of baking powder
- Half cup of chopped sugar-free chocolate

Instructions:

1. Preheat the oven to 170°C/340°F. Grease and line two baking trays with parchment paper.

2. Add the almond meal, collagen protein, salt and baking powder into a bowl.

3. Pour the apple cider vinegar directly on top of the baking powder and allow it to react (it will go fizzy).

4. Add the remaining ingredients to the bowl and stir to combine evenly.

5. Taste the dough and adjust the sweetness if needed.

6. Begin rolling the mixture into balls and place them onto the lined baking tray.

7. Press the balls as flat as you like, they won't rise much, so if you like them softer and chewier keep them quite full. However, if you like a crunchier cookie, press them quite flat using your hands to shape them.

8. Place the cookies in the oven and bake for 15 minutes, or until golden brown.

9. Remove from the oven when they're ready and place the cookies on a wire cooling rack.

10. Store in an airtight jar when completely cooled

76.   Coconut Cookies

Preparation time: 30 minutes   Serving size: 16 cookies

Ingredients:

- Almond flour: 90 g
- Protein (Vanilla): 30 g
- Coconut Flour: 2 tbsp.
- Psyllium: 100 g
- Butter: 30 g
- Sugar Free Chocolate

Preparations

- Combine dry ingredients (flour, protein, psyllium, baking powder).
- Beat room temperature oil with erythritol until fluffy. Add the egg, beat again. after proper beating, add the dry ingredients and mix thoroughly.
- Cut the chocolate into pieces and mix in the dough. Divide the dough into 16 pieces. Roll the balls, put on a baking sheet and press the bottom of the glass to shape.
- Send to the oven preheated to 180 ° C for 10-15 minutes, until golden brown.

77.   Chocolate Chip Cookies

As polls showed, people on a diet most often dream of cookies with pieces of chocolate! Dreams come true. Try this simple and incredibly delicious recipe for homemade cookies with chocolate.

Nutritional value of a serving (a cookie)

- Total calories: 140 calories
- Calories from Fat 108 calories
- Fat: 12 g
- Carbohydrate: 6 g
- Fiber: 4 g
- Digestible Carbohydrate: 2 g
- Protein: 4 g

Preparation time: 30 minutes   Serving size: 16 cookies

Ingredients:

- Almond flour: 90 g
- Protein (Vanilla): 30 g
- Coconut Flour: 2 tbsp.
- Psyllium: 100 g
- Butter: 30 g
- Sugar Free Chocolate

Preparations
- Combine dry ingredients (flour, protein, psyllium, baking powder).
- Beat room temperature oil with erythritol until fluffy. Add the egg, beat again. after proper beating, add the dry ingredients and mix thoroughly.
- Cut the chocolate into pieces and mix in the dough. Divide the dough into 16 pieces. Roll the balls, put on a baking sheet and press the bottom of the glass to shape.
- Send to the oven preheated to 180 ° C for 10-15 minutes, until golden brown.

78.   Keto Sugar Cookies

Preparation time: 20 minutes   Serving size: 8 cookies

Ingredients:
- Almond flour: half cup
- One table spoon Protein
- Two table spoons Coconut Flour
- One table spoon of Butter
- Sugar Free Chocolate

Preparations
- Combine all the dry ingredients (flour, protein baking powder) and mix together.
- Beat room temperature oil with erythritol until fluffy. Add the egg, beat again. after proper beating, add the dry ingredients and mix thoroughly.

- Divide the dough into 16 pieces. Roll the balls, put on a baking sheet and press the bottom of the glass to shape.
- Bake for 180 ° C for 10-15 minutes, until golden brown.

79.   Keto Coconut cookies

Recipe is same as keto sugar cookies. Just add shredded coconut to the batter and mix.

80.   Keto strawberry Cookies

Follow the recipe for keto sugar cookies step by step. Add diced strawberry to the batter and substitute the sugar free chocolate for strawberry powder.

BOMBS

81.   Fat Bombs

Nutritional Value for a bomb

- Total Calories – 120
- Carbohydrate – 1.24 g
- Fat – 3.45 g

Serving size - 10 bombs

Preparation time – 10 minutes

Ingredients

- One cup of cold pressed coconut oil
- Two table spoons of almond butter
- Two table spoons of cocoa powder that is not sweetener
- Two tablespoons of powdered sweetener
- One table spoon of vanilla extract
- A pinch of salt

Preparation

- Put all the ingredients in a mixing bowl and mix until it is smooth,
- Pour into parchment papers and wrap.

Refrigerate until they are hard and solid

82.   Keto buns with oregano

This recipe is as simple to execute as its composition. You don't need to look for rare ingredients to bake delicious keto biscuits with oregano for breakfast. By the way, you can try making keto buns not only with oregano, but also with a mixture of Provencal herbs. This method also turns out very tasty and satisfying. Outside, the pastries have a golden crisp, and inside they are tender and soft, thanks to the addition of olive oil and chicken eggs.

Nutritional value of a serving (1 keto bun):

- Total calories: 131 calories

- Fats: 11 grams.
- Carbohydrates: 1 gram.
- Protein: 7 grams.

Preparation time: 30 minutes   Portion Size: 3 servings (3 buns)

Ingredients:
- oregano buns
- Chicken Egg - 4 pieces
- Olive oil - 4 tablespoons
- Almond flour - 50 gr.
- Salt - ¼ teaspoon
- Oregano or other dried herbs - 1 tablespoon
- Coconut oil (can be replaced with any oil) - to lubricate the mold

Preparation:
- Preheat the oven to 200 ° C;
- Prepare a muffin baking dish. Lubricate it with coke oil;
- Put chicken eggs and olive oil in a deep bowl. Whisk the ingredients with a whisk;
- Add almond flour, salt and oregano to the mixture. Thoroughly mix all the ingredients with a whisk until a homogeneous mass without lumps is obtained;
- Pour the finished dough evenly into the recesses in the baking dish;
- Put the baking dish in the oven for 25 minutes;
- Cool ready-made keto rolls with oregano at room temperature before deciding to remove them from the baking dish. If you get buns earlier, then they can lose their shape.

Why use coconut oil?
It is great for many keto recipes. It is often used for frying due to the fact that when heated, coconut oil does not emit harmful carcinogens. Add a light coconut flavor to the beneficial properties.

83.   Paleo Keto Cinnamon Rolls

Serving size - 10 rolls

Preparation time – 10 minutes

Ingredients

- One cup of cold pressed coconut oil
- Two table spoons of almond butter
- Two table spoons of cinnamon powder
- Two tablespoons of powdered sweetener
- One table spoon of vanilla extract
- A pinch of salt

Preparation

- Put all the ingredients in a mixing bowl and mix until it is smooth,
- Pour into parchment papers and wrap.
- Refrigerate until they are hard and solid

84.   Sweet Keto Breakfast Buns

Nutrients per serving

- Total Calories: 124 calories
- Calories from fat: 74 g
- Fat: 12.06 g
- Protein: 3.68 g
- Carbohydrate: 4.99g

Preparation Time: 50 minutes   Serving size: 12 servings

Ingredients for the Dough:

- Grated mozzarella: 200 gr.
- Curd cheese: 80 gr.

- Chicken egg: 1 piece
- Dough baking powder: ½ teaspoon
- Coconut flour: 120 gr.

Preparation:
- Preheat the oven to 180 ° C;
- Put ground cinnamon, erythritol, walnut, and butter in a blender or food processor. Grind the ingredients until finely moistened crumbs;
- Put cottage cheese and grated mozzarella in a heat-resistant cup. Put the ingredients in the microwave. Warm the cheese until it melts. Remember that mozzarella should not bubble while;
- In a melted cheese mass, put 100 grams of coconut flour, baking powder and chicken egg. Mix all the ingredients thoroughly. Remember that you need to mix foods very quickly before the cheese has time to harden;
- If the cheese dough is too thin and sticky, then add more coconut flour to thicken;
- Roll the dough into a layer with a thickness of 4 mm;
- Lubricate the dough with a sweet filling;
- Divide the dough into 3 cm. Roll each strip you have into the shape of a "snail";
- Take a baking dish and cover it with baking paper. Put future keto rolls in a baking dish;
- Place the baking tray with keto rolls in the oven for 30-35 minutes. The readiness of keto rolls can be determined by the appearance of a golden-brown crust.

85.   Almond Flour Keto Donuts

- Almond flour - One cup
- Sweetener -1/3 cup
- Baking powder - 2 tsp
- One table spoon of cinnamon powder
- A pinch of salt
- Butter - 1/4 cup
- Almond milk of 1/4 cup
- 2 big Eggs
  Half tablespoon of vanilla extract

86.   Keto McMuffin

Honestly, buns are certainly more like pancakes. You can try different variants of keto bread from our recipes, or you can cook these - we like it)

In this recipe, we took ready-made ground beef from grass-fed beef with a fat content of about 10-12%.

Nutritional content of a serving

- Total calories: 538 calories
- Calories from Fat 369
- Fat: 41 g
- Carbohydrates: 3 g

- Fiber: 0 g
- Digestible Carbohydrate: 3 g
- Protein: 37 g

Preparation time: 20 minutes   Serving size: 2

Ingredients

- Egg: 4 pieces
- Parmesan cheese grated: 30 g
- Cream cheese: 100 g
- Salt and spices to taste
- Minced meat: 100g
- Burger Cheese

Preparation:

- Separate the two yolks and mix them with a mixer with Parmesan cheese, cream cheese and a pinch of salt. Set aside. Beat two proteins to steady peaks.
- Gently mix the mixture with the yolks and squirrels.
- If you want your buns to be perfectly round, use a mold.
- Heat the pan over medium heat, pour ¼ of dough and fry for about 2 minutes on each side.
- Meatballs from minced meat and fry in a pan until cooked (about 4 minutes on each side).

- Then, put a piece of cheese on top, pour a tablespoon of water into the pan and hold for a minute under the lid.
- Put the round shape on a cold frying pan, break the egg into it and turn on and turn on the medium heat. When the protein is set from below, mix the yolk, cover and fry until tender.
- Assemble your McMuffin: bun, cutlet, egg, and bun.

87. Low Carb Lemon blueberry donuts

Serving size – 4 doughnuts   Preparation time – 20 minutes

Ingredients

- Two table spoons of lemon juice
- Cream cheese - 90 g
- 3 eggs
- Almond flour - 3 tablespoons
- Coconut flour - one and a half Art. spoons
- Baking powder - half a tablespoon
- Vanilla extract - to taste
- Sweetener - 4 tbsp. tablespoons
- Liquid sweetener - 2 ml

Preparation

- Put all the ingredients in a bowl and mix.
- Then, take an immersion blender and carefully "punch" the dough until a homogeneous consistency is obtained. From experience - you need to work at least a minute and a half with a blender, otherwise lumps may remain
- Heat the waffle iron and brush with coconut oil and only use it for frying, because it does not emit carcinogens at high temperatures
- Bake for 6 minutes, but the time may vary slightly depending on your waffle iron, therefore, for the first three minutes, do not open the lid for sure, and then check that it does not burn.
- Serve when it is done

88.   Coconut Flour Donuts with Chocolate Icing

Follow the steps for the keto doughnuts substituting coconut flour for almond flour.

For the chocolate icing

Mix icing sugar and melted coconut bar together. Top the donuts with the mixture

89.   Sweet Keto Breakfast Buns

Many people love to eat something sweet for breakfast. But we all want the breakfast to be not only healthy, but also delicious. To do this, try to make sweet keto rolls. They have delicious nuts and cinnamon fillings. Therefore, they are somewhat reminiscent of cinnamons. If you and your family love sweet foods for breakfast, then you will definitely like these buns!

Nutrients

- Calories: 124 calories
- Calories from fat: 74 g
- Fat: 12.06 g
- Protein: 3.68 g
- Carbohydrate: 4.99g

Preparation time: 50 minutes   Serving size: 12 servings

Ingredients for the Dough:

- Grated mozzarella: 200 gr.
- Curd cheese: 80 gr.
- Chicken egg: 1 piece
- Dough baking powder: ½ teaspoon
- Coconut flour: 120 gr.

Preparation:

- Preheat the oven to 180 ° C;
- Put ground cinnamon, erythritol, walnut, and butter in a blender or food processor. Grind the ingredients until finely moistened crumbs;

- Put cottage cheese and grated mozzarella in a heat-resistant cup. Put the ingredients in the microwave. Warm the cheese until it melts. Remember that mozzarella should not bubble while;
- In a melted cheese mass, put 100 grams of coconut flour, baking powder and chicken egg. Mix all the ingredients thoroughly. Remember that you need to mix foods very quickly before the cheese has time to harden;
- If the cheese dough is too thin and sticky, then add more coconut flour to thicken;
- Roll the dough into a layer with a thickness of 4 mm;
- Lubricate the dough with a sweet filling;
- Divide the dough into 3 cm. Roll each strip you have into the shape of a "snail";
- Take a baking dish and cover it with baking paper. Put future keto rolls in a baking dish;
- Place the baking tray with keto rolls in the oven for 30-35 minutes. The readiness of keto rolls can be determined by the appearance of a golden-brown crust.

90.   Cinnamon Crumb Cake Keto Donuts

Ingredients
- Two table spoons of cinnamon powder
- Cream cheese - 90 g
- 3 eggs
- Almond flour - 3 tablespoons
- Coconut flour - one and a half Art. spoons
- Baking powder - half a tablespoon
- Vanilla extract - to taste
- Sweetener - 4 tbsp. tablespoons
- Liquid sweetener - 2 ml

Preparation
- Put all the ingredients in a bowl and mix.

- Then, take an immersion blender and carefully "punch" the dough until a homogeneous consistency is obtained. From experience - you need to work at least a minute and a half with a blender, otherwise lumps may remain
- Heat the waffle iron and brush with coconut oil and only use it for frying, because it does not emit carcinogens at high temperatures
- Bake for 6 minutes, but the time may vary slightly depending on your waffle iron, therefore, for the first three minutes, do not open the lid for sure, and then check that it does not burn

91.   Keto Doughnuts

Ingredients
- Cream cheese - 90 g
- 3 eggs
- Almond flour - 3 tablespoons
- Coconut flour - one and a half Art. spoons
- Baking powder - half a tablespoon
- Vanilla extract - to taste
- Sweetener - 4 tbsp. tablespoons
- Liquid stevia - 2 ml

Preparation
- Put all the ingredients in a bowl and mix.
- Then, take an immersion blender and carefully "punch" the dough until a homogeneous consistency is obtained. From experience - you need to work at least a minute and a half with a blender, otherwise lumps may remain
- Heat the waffle iron and brush with coconut oil and only use it for frying, because it does not emit carcinogens at high temperatures
- Bake for 6 minutes, but the time may vary slightly depending on your waffle iron, therefore, for the first three minutes, do not open the lid for sure, and then check that it does not burn

- Grease the donuts with low-calorie syrup and laid out slices of fried bacon. So, for beauty).

92.   Mozzarella

Nutrients:

- Calories: 257 Cal
- Carbohydrate: 4.7 g
- Fiber: 1.1 g

- Digestible Carbohydrates: 3.5 g
- Protein: 17.3 g.

Preparation time: 30 minutes

Serving size: 8 servings

Ingredients:

- Mozzarella cheese: 100 g
- Cream cheese: 30 g
- Almond flour: 1 cup
- Egg: 1 piece
- Beef sausage: 8 pcs

Preparation:

- Grate the cheese on a coarse grater
- In a bowl, combine Mozzarella, cream cheese and flour. Microwave for 30 seconds
- Beat the egg and mix thoroughly.
- The dough should have a dense consistency
- Put your dough between two sheets of sides and roll it
- Cut the dough into 8 strips using the pizza wheel
- Gently wrap the sausages in the dough and place on a baking sheet. Put in the oven preheated to 200 C for 20-25 minutes, until a golden crust appears.

93.   Swedish Meatball:

Ingredients:
- Zucchini grated: 1 tbsp.
- Egg: 1 pc
- Minced meat.

Preparations:
- Combine both minced meat in a large bowl.
- Grate zucchini and add to the minced meat without removing excess water.
- Break the egg into the minced meat, add salt and pepper. Shuffle everything with your hands.
- Melt the butter in a cast-iron skillet with a thick bottom. Form from the meat mixture not too large (as in the picture) balls of equal size.
- Fry the balls properly for 3-5 minutes on either side until they turn golden brown.

In a separate bowl, mix the broth, mustard and cream until smooth. Pour the mixture into a meatball pan and simmer for 5-10 minutes until the sauce has hardened.

CONCLUSION

So, here we have them, Keto dessert recipes for the sweet lovers out there to maintain ketosis and lose weight while still enjoying the simple pleasures of life. In following a diet, an important attitude to have is one of discipline and diligence. Hence, you should not slack or give up as you go on this journey.

All the best.

Made in the USA
Monee, IL
14 September 2020

42541509R00057